READING THE ENEMY'S MAIL:

ORIGINS AND DEVELOPMENT OF
U.S. ARMY TACTICAL
RADIO INTELLIGENCE
IN WORLD WAR II,
EUROPEAN THEATER OF OPERATIONS

by

JEFFREY S. HARLEY, MAJ, USA

U.S. Army Command and General Staff College

Fort Leavenworth, Kansas

1993

Table of Contents

Foreword

This book traces the development of American radio intelligence at the operational and tactical levels from its beginnings in World War I through the end of World War II. It shows that signals intelligence is useful to the tactical and operational level commander. The study recommends the Army rethink signal intelligence support to the various echelons, primarily through changes to tables of organization and equipment.

The thesis covers the initial appearance of radio intelligence units on the battlefields of France in the first world war, identifying specific instances where radio intelligence played a role in a command decision. It also looks at training and doctrine in the period between the two world wars. The thesis also covers the organization, doctrine, and training of radio intelligence units as they prepared for combat. It provides a glimpse into the intelligence support provided to the corps, army, and army group commanders during World War II through examination of actual intercept operations. Where possible the study compares and contrasts German radio intelligence units and operations with their American counterparts.

Acknowledgments

I want to take this opportunity to thank those who assisted me in completing this work. Thanks to LTC Connelly and Dr. Lewis for guiding and instructing me in the ways of historical research, and keeping me on track throughout the entire process. Thanks to LTC Sower for reminding me to keep the focus of "so what" up front as I researched.

I thank COL Dickson Gribble for implanting in a young captain the spark to delve further into a chosen profession. His example inspired me to learn more about the Army and the Military Intelligence branch.

Finally, my deepest thanks to my wife and children, who probably often wondered how this could possibly have been the best year of their lives.

The opinions and conclusions expressed herein are those of the student author and do not necessarily represent the views of the U.S. Army Command and General Staff College or any other governmental agency.

2

CHAPTER ONE - INTRODUCTION

In late August 1914 the majority of the German Army attacked into Belgium and Northern France. Left to defend the eastern front was General Max von Prittwitz and the German Eighth Army. Two Russian armies, the First under General Pavel K. Rennenkampf and the Second under General Aleksandr Samsonov in the north and south respectively, attacked into German territory. Failing to halt the Russian First Army, General von Prittwitz contemplated evacuating East Prussia, withdrawing across the Vistula River. The Kaiser consequently replaced him with General Paul von Hindenburg.

Von Hindenburg adopted a plan to entrap and destroy Samsonov's Second Army. Leaving a screen to confront Rennenkampf's army, von Hindenburg began to concentrate his forces in the south. Five days later he halted, then encircled and destroyed the Second Army near Tannenberg. The Second Army broke and lost nearly 125,000 men and 500 guns from 26 to 31 August. Von Hindenburg then turned his attention to the north, concentrated against the First Army, and drove it out of East Prussia. In this campaign, the Germans lost about 10,000 men while inflicting losses that exceeded 250,000 for the Russians. General von Hindenburg fought a brilliant defensive campaign using aggressive offensive tactics. The United States Army still uses the Battle of Tannenberg as an example of achieving a defensive goal through use of aggressive offensive tactics.[1] The Battle of Tannenberg also illustrates the importance of radio intelligence in operational maneuver. Without prior knowledge of the enemy's intentions, it is doubtful General von Hindenburg would have been willing to take the risks that he did.[2]

The purpose of this paper is to examine the influence of radio intelligence at the army, corps, and army group level in World War II. How was radio intelligence used at the operational and tactical levels during World War II? How did American radio intelligence compare to German units and operations? What lessons did we learn, and what is the effect of those lessons on today's forces?

At every echelon, division, corps, and theater army, there are military intelligence (MI) units with the sole purpose of providing signals intelligence support to the commander. One Combat Electronic Warfare and Intelligence (CEWI) battalion directly supports a division; two MI battalions (the Technical Exploitation and the Aerial Exploitation) support a corps; and two MI Battalions (SIGINT) support theater armies worldwide. The roots of these units can be found in the radio intelligence and signal service companies from World War II.

No classified material was used in the thesis. While simplifying research, classification problems arose in an unexpected arena. It appears that few operational records (those with actual intercept logs, message contents, etc.) were saved after the war. Two units, after writing their after action reports, destroyed their operational logs because of security reasons, but also to reduce the amount of baggage to take home. This created a gap in tracing how any intercepted material became intelligence briefed to a commander.

Adding to this gap was the lack of discussion concerning signals intelligence in World War II until the late 1970's. People directly involved with radio intelligence, whether with ULTRA or at the operational level, kept quiet for over 30 years. In his book, Brigadier General Oscar Koch, Patton's G-2, mentions the use of radio intelligence several times during the North African campaign. After that there is nothing written that indicates his use of radio intelligence during the western European campaigns.[3]

Worse than the lack of material concerning American radio intelligence is the lack of material, in English, concerning German radio intelligence. I had to rely on two sources for information on the Germans.[4] Wherever possible I have attempted to compare German operations to American operations.

All of the sources used can be found in the Combined Arms Research Library (CARL), Bell Hall, at Fort Leavenworth, Kansas. The bibliography identifies the file numbers of the government documents used which may not be easily available to the general public. The books cited in the bibliography can be found in, or readily obtained by, most libraries.

ULTRA will not be discussed in any great detail within this paper, as it has been covered extensively elsewhere. Those interested in ULTRA, its use at the army group and army level, and the Special Liaison Units (SLUs) are invited to read Colonel Gribble's excellent study.[5]

Leaders have always sought knowledge about their enemy. Sun Tzu's admonition to "know thy enemy and know thyself; in a hundred battles you will never be in peril"[6] remains as true today as it did thousands of years ago. Before the advent of radio, commanders relied mostly on spies or their own troops for intelligence concerning the enemy and his location. The telegraph gave senior commanders the ability to provide orders over greater distances and control several theaters, but it could not be effectively used at the operational and tactical level. Radio, as technology progressed and systems became smaller, began to be used to control armies and corps. In World War I, several nations incorporated radio communications into their maneuvers. Today it is impossible to envision deploying any type of force without some type of radio communication back to its parent headquarters.

This paper begins the story of radio intelligence from its inception in World War I, then covers its development during the inter-war period from 1919 to 1938. Chapter two discusses the state of doctrine, organization, and training of American radio intelligence companies at the outbreak of World War II. Chapter three looks at how units modified the doctrine based on their wartime experience. Chapter four provides an overview of actual radio intelligence operations by looking at two radio intelligence units, one at army level, the other at corps. Chapter five contains the analysis and any conclusions or lessons that can be applied to today's army. Before looking at the units and their contribution in World War II, it is necessary to begin at the start of radio interception and its usage: the Battle of Tannenberg.

World War I (1914-1918)

Germany

The story behind Hindenburg's bold moves lies in the intelligence he received from radio intercept. When war broke out, the Germans had no fixed organization for intercepting foreign army radio traffic. The German telegraph field regulations foresaw the possibility of listening in on foreign traffic when their own radio traffic was dormant. Telegraph troops could gain insight into the situation of the other side through eavesdropping on non-German communications. In reality this was never done in peacetime, and when the war broke out, nobody thought of undertaking the task.

The Russians used the radio to communicate between the armies and corps. Wire was their primary means of communication, but the advance into Prussia stretched their resources to the breaking point. The movement of the two Russian armies crossed the Masurian lakes region, separating them by 40 miles. The two armies could only communicate with each other by radio. Radios were fairly new and were just becoming integrated into military organizations.[7]

On 20 August 1914, Rennenkampf radioed to Samsonov that he was halting his advance for three days so that his supply trains could catch up. German airplane and cavalry reconnaissance confirmed the intercepted message.[8] To avoid delays and errors inherent in encrypting and decrypting messages, Samsonov had the orders to his corps, detailing their dispositions and lines of march for the next day, 25 August 1917, transmitted in clear text. That day, the Germans also intercepted Rennenkampf's orders to his army that gave his marching distances and objectives. Rennenkampf's message showed that the Germans did not have to worry about their rear, while they massed for their attack on Samsonov's Second Army.[9] No military commander had been granted such an intelligence coup since MG McClellan captured a copy of General Lee's orders prior to the Battle of Antietam in 1862.[10]

At that time there were two large radio stations in East Prussia, Konigsberg and Thorn. Entirely on their own initiative, a few operators began to listen to Russian radio traffic during lulls. The radio station at the German fortress of Konigsberg intercepted several of these messages through sheer chance. No one knew what to do with the first few intercepted radio messages, because there was no regulation stating what should be done. The Russian operational orders given to Hindenburg prior to Tannenberg were forwarded solely on the personal initiative of the Thorn radio station chief.[11] They disclosed the intentions of the Russian forces moving into East Prussia in such detail that Hindenburg gained an unprecedented knowledge of enemy intentions.

After Tannenberg, the German High Command, *Oberste Heersleitung* (OHL), established radio intercept posts. Both Austrian and German intercept stations were able to keep their forces current on Russian plans for the remainder of the war. Wilhelm Flicke estimated that in view of the existing force ratios, it was impossible for the Austro- German offensive in 1915 to succeed as it did without access to Russian intentions. By September 1915, the war in the east became deadlocked across a 950 mile front.[12]

In the west it was a different story. The Germans did not appreciate the lessons learned against the Russians. The German plan envisioned advancing through Belgium, thrusting towards Paris. Once the attack began, the Germans started using radio to control and monitor their forces. Because of the lack of radio intercept experience before the war, little communications security (COMSEC), if any, was practiced. Call signs and frequencies did not change, and radio stations within the same organization used the same letter as the beginning of their call sign.[13]

The French had built their own intercept service.

Because of German mistakes, it became easy for the French to develop the German's order of battle, track their forces as they moved, and determine their intent. The payoff came at the Battle of the Marne, where the French halted the German attack.[1,4]

United States

When the United States entered the war in 1917, it was inevitable that its services would become involved in radio intelligence. In 1916, a mobile direction finding and intercept van accompanied General John J. "Blackjack" Pershing during the Mexican punitive expedition against Pancho Villa. The three mobile "radio tractors" were used to monitor Mexican government communications.[15]

The American Expeditionary Forces (AEF) in France fielded two units with the same name, the Radio Intelligence Section. One section belonged to the Radio Intelligence Section, General Staff, commonly known then as "G-2, A-6." It concerned itself primarily with attacking German codes and ciphers. The other section was the Radio Intelligence Section, Signal Corps, later referred to as Radio Section of the Radio Division, Signal Corps. This section performed the intercept and goniometric (direction finding) functions.[16]

The AEF organized the Radio Division of the Office of the Chief Signal Officer on 17 October 1917. It wrote the operating regulations, and determined radio call signs, frequency allocation, and radio net assignments. The division also published circulars and instructions for radio operations and the training of personnel. The radio section within the radio division was also responsible for the radio intercept stations. This section worked very closely with the radio intelligence section of the General Staff, G-2.[17]

The radio section began the war with two officers and 53 enlisted men. By the end of the war their strength was 12 officers and 402 soldiers. Training for the most part was conducted at French schools. The AEF established its first radio intercept station at Souilly on 8 December 1917, colocated with the headquarters of the 2d French Army. The first wire intercept station deployed in February 1918 with the 1st U.S. Division in the St. Mihiel salient.[18]

The Signal Corps opened the radio intercept station at Souilly with one sergeant and eight men of the Second Field Signal Battalion. Maintaining twenty four hour coverage, the station intercepted 393 messages by the end of the month.[19] In December 1917, 54 men arrived from the United States for assignment to the radio intelligence section of the Signal Corps.

After undergoing a five week training program, only 15 of the men were actually assigned to radio intercept duties. The others were assigned to wire intercept, an activity that usually provided more information in the static trench warfare.[20]

The radio intelligence section was also responsible for wire intercept operations. The first wire intercept station was established in February 1918 with the 1st U.S. Division in the St. Mihiel salient.[21] The wire intercept service was usually a dangerous job. Soldiers had to go into no-man's land to install their search wires, near or in direct contact with the enemy's wires. Artillery fire from both sides often created breaks in the lines, thus requiring teams to go back into no-man's land for repair.[22]

Radio intercept, on the other hand, was neither hazardous nor readily transparent to the enemy. One could be some distance behind the front lines and still be effective. By October 1918 both the First and Second US Army headquarters fielded radio intercept stations.[23] From the date the first intercept was received at General Headquarters, messages came in so fast that G-2 personnel were unable to handle them all and it became necessary to increase the section. The G-2, A-6 section obtained additional people from all available sources: divisions, replacement depots, Washington DC, and so forth.

They searched for those who knew German, but they encountered much difficulty. The growth of the G-2 section stimulated the Signal Corps to assign additional personnel to interception work. By the time the AEF took over its section of the lines, there was considerable experience in radio intelligence.[24]

The Signal Corps radio intelligence section performed the technical work of observing the enemy's communications. Radio-goniometric stations located enemy radio stations by bearings. These stations measured, within approximately two degrees, the direction the enemy's signals came from. The intersection of these lines from three or more radio-goniometric stations produced a fix, from which an accurate location could be obtained.[25] The primary duty of the goniometric stations was to daily locate all enemy stations and determine the divisional, corps, and army nets. By locating the stations, and determining their relationship through net protocol, the enemy's order of battle could be developed.[26]

Intercept stations along the army front listened continuously for enemy radio messages. These stations were directly connected with wire to the G-2, A-6, and intercepted messages were telegraphed in directly for decoding and interpretation.[27]

During the St. Mihiel operation, radio intelligence played a key role in American operations. Late in the evening of 24 August 1918, the radio intercept service intercepted and relayed a German message to the AEF's G-2, A-6, where it was immediately deciphered. The message ordered an attack to begin at 0100 the following morning. A warning reached the American lines 30 minutes before the attack began. Later the AEF G-2 began a study of enemy communications within the St. Mihiel salient to detect any changes in organization or procedure that might reveal the enemy's intentions. On 8 September they spotted a change. The activity of enemy radio stations increased for the next three days, leading the Americans to believe that the Germans were wary of a surprise attack and were withdrawing from the salient. On 11 September, the day before the AEF attacked, reports received from goniometric stations disclosed that all enemy radio stations were in their normal locations and in operation, the enemy had not withdrawn. In spite of all other indications, the G-2, based on information provided by the radio section, could positively show that the enemy remained within the salient.[28] The radio intelligence officer (G-2, A-6) of the AEF wrote as follows to the effectiveness of American direction finding during the St. Mihiel drive:

15

Just before the American attack on the St. Mihiel Salient there were many indications that the enemy had withdrawn and the advisability of advancing the infantry without artillery preparation was seriously considered. The final decision to make the attack as originally planned was based on the evidence of the goniometric service that the enemy radio stations were still active in their old locations.[29]

Beginning with unplanned, uncoordinated occasional radio intercepts at the Battle of Tannenberg, the usefulness of radio intercept came to be recognized by all the powers in the conflict. The World War I achievements of German radio intelligence, initially improvised and later systematically developed, made it appear necessary for the *Reichswehr* to utilize this experience and, in spite of all restrictions, to provide such facilities as would encourage and promote this activity.[30]

Not all countries would heed this lesson from the war to end all wars. A recommendation from LTC Frank Moorman, Chief of the G-2, A-6 section, stated that

> There should be organized and maintained at all times a complete unit of the Radio Intelligence Section which should serve as a training school for officers and men and permit of experiments for improvement of this service. The necessary Signal Corps personnel should be provided and work actually conducted on a small scale, along the lines contemplated during a state of war.[31.]

Inter-war period (1918-1938)

Germany

After Versailles, Germany remembered the lesson learned at Tannenberg. The military clauses of the Versailles Treaty provided that the seven infantry and three cavalry divisions of the *Reichswehr*, whose strength was limited to 100,000 men, would be allowed seven divisional signal battalions, each comprising two companies, one of which was to include an intercept platoon. In addition, the Germans were permitted to assign signal personnel to schools, garrisons, and headquarters and to maintain twelve major military radio stations at military district headquarters.[32] The treaty did not, however, provide for any communication intelligence units.[33]

Realizing that intelligence was of particular importance to an army restricted in strength and equipment, the German military leaders decided that the radio intelligence operations initiated during World War I should be continued and further developed. These activities were given the official designation Intercept Service.[34] During the second half of 1921 the officers in charge of the stations received specific orders to monitor certain foreign radio channels. The stations in Muenster,

Hanover, Kassel, Stuttgart, Nuernberg, and Munich intercepted British and French traffic, while those in Stettin, Breslau, Dresden, Frankfurt an der Oder, and Konigsberg observed primarily Polish, Russian, and Czechoslovak traffic. The advisor to the senior signal officer on the staff of the corps headquarters in Berlin and Kassel was in control of communication intelligence operations. These two officers reported directly to the Signal Inspectorate of the *Reichswehr* Ministry whenever they obtained information of special interest.[35]

At first the Germans merely intended to gather information about foreign military procedures as a basis for traffic analysis, including such elements as frequencies, call signs, operating signals, radio procedures, and equipment. Only later did their analysis begin to develop order of battle data by evaluating radio station relationships. No provisions had yet been made for text analysis, i.e., the translation of foreign language messages to plain text and the solution of encrypted messages.[36]

In 1925 the Intercept Service established six intercept stations at Konigsberg, Frankfurt an der Oder, Breslau, Stuttgart, Muenster, and Munich. The personnel strength of each station was one officer, three noncommissioned officers, fifteen male and five female radio operators, and three translators. The stations were generally equipped with sensitive receivers covering a frequency range of from 100 to 3000 kilocycles (kc). The intercept operations were to be kept completely separate from those of the radio stations, and they were located in different buildings.[37]

Each intercept station was to cover certain countries in established priority ratings. An area which was given top priority was covered by at least two stations, which exchanged their results. Interception was no longer confined to military traffic, but was extended to all radio communications, except naval, for which the German Navy had established its own communication intelligence agency. The army became more and more interested in diplomatic radio traffic, since it provided the only material for the analysis of difficult cryptosystems.[38]

The Germans continued to place emphasis on the observation of the radio traffic of foreign armies for the purpose of ascertaining their organization, strength, and distribution of forces. In this connection the observation of foreign maneuvers assumed great significance, and direction finding training was stressed to develop a detailed picture of troop maneuvers. The Intercept Service observed the British maneuvers in the Rhineland in 1928, Czech and Polish maneuvers in 1929, and French maneuvers from 1930 onwards. Flicke observed that the intercept results from some of the exercises were more comprehensive than the reports of the military attaches and agents employed.[39]

After 1928 German signal experts focused on short wave traffic. They studied the effectiveness of short waves at all hours of the day and night, as well as under different weather conditions. From 1930 they plotted medium wave transmitting stations operating between 1000 and 3000 kc. In 1931 automatic high speed reception was introduced employing wax disk, tape, and other sound recorders.[40]

The observation of maneuvers from fixed baselines led to the idea of using mobile equipment for intercept operations. In 1930 the Germans began to develop special trucks for radio receiving, direction finding, and evaluation units. The signal unit of the Artillery School tested the new equipment. The tests proved that intercept units could keep up with the fast moving action of a meeting engagement, provided the necessary communications for relaying the results could be established. Directing this work was first the Cipher Center and then the Main Intercept Post, a new command organized around 1936.[41]

United States

In the United States the intercept service which supported the combat forces in France quickly disbanded after the war. Of the 80 men who served in the radio intelligence section of the G-2, only five remained on active duty by 2 January 1919.[42] However, the volume of intercepts of foreign diplomatic messages grew considerably, and so did American collection operations. Throughout the inter-war period the State Department, Army Signal Corps, and Navy Department each had separate intercept and cryptoanalytic facilities. In 1929 Henry L. Stimson, Secretary of State, withdrew funding for his department's intercept activities, stating "Gentlemen do not read each other's mail."[43]

In addition to expanding their individual service intelligence efforts, the War Department and the State Department also cooperated to form the nation's first peacetime cryptological organization, the Black Chamber. In May 1919, the director of the Military Intelligence Division (MID) sent a memo to the Army Chief of Staff proposing a permanent organization to break codes and ciphers. The memo recommended funding of $100,000 annually, with the State Department supplying $40,000 and the Army $60,000. Both organizations approved the plan, and by July 1919 State

21

Department funds began flowing to the new organization. The War Department began funding the Black Chamber in June 1921.[44]

Initially, the Black Chamber made several notable successes, the most well known being its breaking of the Japanese diplomatic code. During the 1921 Washington Naval Conference, the Black Chamber provided daily solutions to Japanese messages detailing their positions on the talks. Forearmed with this information, the American negotiators could take a tougher stand to get the results desired.

Despite its successes, the Black Chamber only received the full $100,000 in 1920. The following year the War Department reduced its contribution from $60,000 to $10,000, claiming it only provided information useful to the State Department. By 1929 hardly any War Department funds went to the Black Chamber.[45]

Besides funding problems, the Black Chamber also ran into intercept problems. During World War I, the Signal Corps operated radio intercept stations and commercial cable companies gave the government copies of all messages passing through their offices. In 1920 the Signal Corps closed its last main wartime intercept station in Maine. This, coupled with demobilization of the radio units in France, led to no intercept capability in the army, whether strategic or tactical. Later legislation passed in the 1920s made it illegal to provide copies of messages to secondary sources, thus completely drying up the source of material for the Black Chamber.[46]

However, the problems of the Black Chamber led to a study of possible alternatives. In April 1929 the army's chief of staff agreed with the suggestion to place all cryptological activities under the Chief Signal Officer. The new Signal Intelligence Service (SIS) had five objectives: code compilation, code and cipher solution, radio intercept, goniometry (direction finding), and secret inks. Soon after the creation of the SIS, the Signal Corps established six foreign interception stations.[47] As tensions increased in Europe, the SIS would be one of the first organizations to increase its strength. Early 1939 saw the creation of the Second Signal battalion to command the radio intercept companies and platoons involved in strategic communications intelligence activities.[48]

CHAPTER TWO - ORGANIZATION AND DOCTRINE

As mentioned in the previous chapter, the Chief Signal Officer was responsible for all codes and cipher work in the army. *Army Regulation 105-5,* dated 10 May 1929, formally established the Signal Intelligence Service. The 1930's saw the Signal Corps assume responsibility for conducting signals intelligence within the War Department. In this period, the Signal Corps emphasized strategic level intercept, mainly intercept and decoding of Japanese communications. Both the Navy and the Army focused their efforts in this direction. By 1935 the Army's Signal Intelligence Service (SIS), under the leadership of William F. Friedman, broke the *Angooki Taipu A,* or Type A cipher machine used by Japanese naval attaches. In September 1940 the SIS solved the newer Type B cipher machine, code-named PURPLE.[49] Neglected during this period was radio intelligence support in the field. The manning, training, and equipping of tactical radio intelligence companies would not get well under way until late in World War II. In contrast, the strategic SIS functions had been highly organized and effective from the very start of the war.[50]

The wartime activities of the SIS would be carried out at the War Department, General Headquarters, and at

Headquarters of Field Armies levels.[51] From its beginning until 1939, the SIS had been an activity focused solely at the War Department level, little had been done to develop or improve SIS capabilities at the general headquarters or field army levels.[52] This neglect would leave the Signal Corps ill prepared to perform one of its wartime functions: providing radio intelligence to the field commander.

In October 1939 the Third Radio Intelligence Company, one of the first tactically oriented radio intelligence units, was activated at Fort Monmouth. A cadre of eleven men, plus one recruit and an officer, formed the nucleus of the company. By November the company reached full strength and began an intensive four week training program. The problems the unit faced in training would beset new units throughout the war.[53]

Organization and Doctrine - 1940

At the beginning of World War II, Table of Organization (T/O) 77 and Field Manual (FM) 11-20 provided the organization and operations of the radio intelligence company. The radio intelligence company was an organic part of the army and GHQ signal service. As such, it functioned under the command of the chief signal officer. Besides supporting an army or GHQ, a radio intelligence company doctrinally could also be employed in support of American coastal or other frontier defenses, or within the zone of the interior (continental United States).[54]

The primary duties of the radio intelligence company were to:

- Establish, operate, and maintain radio stations to obtain signals intelligence by intercepting, and locating through direction finding, enemy radio stations;

- Obtain information relating to signal security by intercepting friendly radio transmissions; and,

- Obtain information on unauthorized radio stations through intercept and direction finding.

Additional duties were to:

- Install, operate, and maintain the company's wire system;

- Promptly transmit all signal intelligence and information to the army or GHQ headquarters; and,

- Recommend actions to be taken or procedures to be followed to improve friendly signal security.[55]

Organization

A radio intelligence company had to be capable of operating 20 intercept stations on a 24 hour schedule under war conditions. Four intercept stations made one intercept section.

Each operations platoon had one section, and the company headquarters platoon had two. Each company also had 12 direction finding stations to operate on an army frontage of approximately 35 miles. Again, stations were grouped by fours into a position finding section, one section per operating platoon. Each operating platoon had three sections: the intercept section, the control section, and the position finding (direction finding) section.[56]

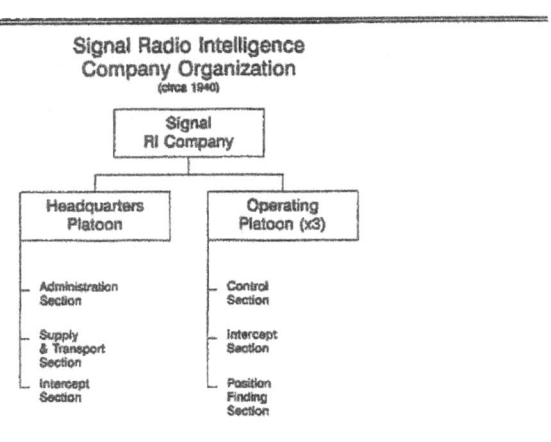

Figure 1. Doctrinal Signal Radio Intelligence Company organization (Source: FM 11-20, page 44)

The platoon leader, through the control section, assigned missions to the intercept and direction finding sections. The plotting team received the lines of bearing (LOBS) from the direction finding stations, and plotted the data on a map to determine the location of the transmitter. The wire team installed the wire and telephones to the DF stations and an administration team which assembled and forwarded the collected data to the proper recipients.

The intercept section of the operating platoons ran 24 hour missions. Each section had a chief and two shifts with four radio operators each, a total of nine men. Its mission was to conduct search and guard missions. To search, a radio operator constantly rolled through the frequency spectrum looking for enemy or unknown transmissions. A guard mission required an operator to keep his receiver on one frequency at all times. The operator maintained a constant watch on this frequency, copied or recorded all transmissions, and passed the collected data to the control section.[57]

The position finding section received missions and targets from the control section. This section operated the direction finding equipment and reported azimuths (lines of bearings) back to the control section. The position finding section consisted of a section chief, assistant section chief, and four DF teams. A team chief and three radio operators comprised one DF team.[58]

Doctrine

FM 11-20 identified how the operations of the radio intelligence company would be effected in varying degrees by tactical operations. When the supported force was in an assembly area, or conducting a march where enemy contact is not expected, the intercept and control section were used. The focus would be more on friendly signal security, specifically cryptographic security, than on interception of enemy communications. During movement to contact and the meeting engagement, the radio intelligence company would first deploy the intercept sections to monitor enemy transmissions, and if the situation permitted, establish the direction finding operations. If DF operations could be initiated, then one platoon would establish the initial baseline, and the other two platoons would leapfrog and establish subsequent baselines. In this manner the company provided continuous direction finding support.[59]

In a stabilized or defensive situation, where little movement was expected, all elements of the RI company were deployed and operated. The intercept teams in the headquarters platoon would provide friendly SIGSEC and guard specific enemy frequencies. The intercept sections from the operating platoons conducted search operations to obtain additional intelligence. Direction finding operations were conducted since movement of enemy stations could indicate a change in the enemy's posture, dispositions, or intent.[60]

The radio intelligence company would also support offensive operations. In a limited attack, the company's intercept teams were to move as far forward towards the front as possible and continue with normal operations. In a large scale offensive, the company could weight the main effort by providing two or more platoons in primary support. By using the leapfrogging method described above, continuous collection operations could be maintained through successive displacements. If the friendly attack was successful, the enemy's wire system would be disrupted and he would be forced to use his radios to control his forces. Intercept and DF operations assumed greater importance during these exploitation and pursuit operations.[61]

The radio intelligence company would be required to cover an army's frontage in a stabilized situation. This roughly equated to a frontage of 20 to 25 miles with a depth of 20 miles. Doctrinally, the operating platoons were to be normally established within 3000 yards of the front line.

At this distance the length of the platoon's DF baseline did not exceed ten miles from end to end. If the platoon established itself farther back from the front line, then the baseline length grew longer. For example, if the platoon was seven to twelve miles behind the front, the DF baseline would extend 20 to 25 miles.[62]

American staff officers learned to place instructions pertaining to the radio intelligence company in paragraph 3 of the signal annex or intelligence annex, in operational orders, or conveyed by messages. The messages containing the missions or results desired would be transmitted to the signal intelligence service of the headquarters to which the company was assigned. The company commander would determine how the company organized and assigned missions to produce the desired results. He was expected to be familiar with the general situation, disposition of friendly forces from army to division level, the signal system, and any other pertinent data necessary to perform the mission. A key contact would be the signal intelligence service, which was to maintain close contact with the supported G-2.

Doctrine and Organization, Post 1940

As the Army gained experience in conducting signal intelligence operations, it began to change its pre-war doctrine. By 1945 the duties of the radio intelligence company at army level were simplified to obtaining intelligence by intercepting enemy communications, and obtaining information on unauthorized radio stations. It also became apparent that signal intelligence units did not have the resources to do both missions simultaneously, thus placing more importance on the signal officers and G-2 to use these resources wisely.[63]

Also at the army level was a Signal Intelligence subsection of the Signal Section, Army Headquarters.[64] The subsection generally consisted of administrative, radio intelligence, security, and solution subgroups. The radio intelligence subgroup recommended actions to all subordinate radio intelligence units to ensure optimum employment of assets. The solution subgroup did not perform original cryptanalysis, but concentrated instead on deciphering messages with solutions provided by the War Department's Signal Intelligence Service.[65]

As the war progressed, the need for a radio intercept capability to support corps and division commanders became evident. Initially the table of organization and equipment for a signal company assigned one radio intercept platoon per division. However, the practice did not fit with the theory. During the Third Army's 1943 maneuvers in Tennessee, both participating divisions, the 85th and the 93rd, had their own RI platoon. From a signals intelligence standpoint, the maneuvers were a disaster.

One Signal Corps observer, Colonel Gillette, stated that the radio intelligence platoons were trained as far as possible considering their lack of equipment. Practically no intercept or direction finding work was done during the exercise. Instead, the signal company commanders used the RI personnel to form additional wire sections. Colonel Gillette observed that both platoons were of little or no value without equipment.[66]

Each RI platoon only had two pieces of DF equipment, obsolete SCR-206s, instead of the ten intercept receivers and three direction finders required. Lack of equipment was so severe that the 85th Signal Company borrowed one SCR-206 and used their own funds to buy the second.[67] The G-2 of the 85th Division stated that the RI platoon had done absolutely nothing and that even if they had had equipment, he considered radio intercept unnecessary.

The radio intercept platoon of the 29th Signal Company, 29th Infantry Division, encountered other problems. The table of organization did not identify the owner of equipment by section, consequently the various sections and platoons struggled for the new equipment when it arrived. The signal company also did not understand the mission of the radio platoon, since it was incompatible with the company's overall mission of providing communications for the division. The platoon had to retain all personnel assigned to it, since incoming personnel were assigned to a signal division and not necessarily to intercept work.

The problems suffered by the radio intelligence platoons of the 29th, 85th, and 93rd Signal Companies were indicative of the problems of trying to provide intercept and direction finding support to echelons below army level. It became impossible to operate a radio intelligence activity as part of a divisional signal company because of the divergence of their respective missions. In mid 1943 the Signal Corps switched to T/O&E 11-500, under which Signal Service companies would be organized to provide radio intelligence to a corps commander. T/O&E 11-500 provided 54 cellular organizations that could be combined into a composite unit to satisfy a theater's requirements. By the end of the war, the number of teams included in this T/O increased to 116. Under the cellular concept, teams or sections could be added or subtracted as needed, thus eliminating duplication in some of the older T/O's.[68]

By 1945 a doctrinal shift took place in the Signal Corps regarding radio intelligence. Prior to the war, doctrine provided for radio intelligence support at army and higher echelons. Shortly after the war began, the army recognized the need for radio intelligence support at corps level. FM 11-22 rewrote doctrine by including two radio intelligence platoons in the corps signal battalion to perform signal intelligence functions. The corps directly controlled the platoons' operations. The G-2 was responsible for signal intelligence activities within the corps. The corps' signal officer had the responsibility for the technical training and tactical employment of all signal units.[69]

Also contained within the corps' signal battalion was the traffic analysis section. This section worked with the corps G-2, signal officer, and the army intelligence service to analyze enemy communications. The information from the radio intelligence platoons would be evaluated by this section and the intelligence provided to the G-2. The section would be concerned with lower echelon enemy communications.[70]

In Europe, the Signal Corps organized Signal Service companies to provide radio intelligence support to a corps. The nucleus of these companies came from the radio intelligence platoons in the divisional signal companies. The platoon from the 29th Division became the 3250th Signal Service Company assigned to V Corps. Other similar units formed within the European Theater of Operations were the 3251st, 3253rd,

3254th, 3255th, 3256th and 3259th Signal Service Companies.

The 3254th provides an example of the general organization of the signal service company. It was composed of a company headquarters team, two platoon headquarters teams, one radio intelligence platoon traffic analysis unit, two radio intercept teams, one radio direction finder team, plus the ancillary mess, message center, teletype and maintenance teams. The composition of the teams under T/O&E 11-500 gave the unit an authorized strength of eight officers and 121 enlisted men, with the initial cadre reassigned from the 59th Signal Battalion. The company fielded three platoons, one headquarters platoon, one communications platoon, and one radio intelligence platoon.[71]

Training

The training of US Army tactical radio intelligence units in 1940 was not as complete or efficient as desired. As men were called up and units activated, schools began without complete programs of instruction. Captain W.D. Hamlin, 3rd Radio Intelligence Company commander, remarked that the training program at Fort Monmouth, New Jersey, began with an intensive four week program based on a Signal Corps School pamphlet. After finishing this training, the company began morse code training with instructors resorting to loudspeakers to relay the information. Later code recorders and transmitters arrived, greatly facilitating training.[72]

In early 1940 the 3rd Radio Intelligence Company began receiving its equipment and started training on radio operating, radio intercept, and direction finding principles. The unit suffered from not enough space to establish nets for direction finding operations, lack of targets for intercept operations, and lack of transport to move into the field. By March 1940 only 65% of the men could copy morse code by hand at a rate greater than eight words per minute (wpm). When they reached 12 wpm, training began on using typewriters to copy traffic. Other units would face the same problems later, as the mobilization pace increased and the United States went to war.[73]

The 116th Radio Intelligence Company, activated at Camp Crowder, Missouri on 18 May 1942, began with a cadre of 14 soldiers and one officer. The cadre came from the 125th Radio Intelligence. Company at Fort Lewis, Washington. The signal corps often had to transfer trained personnel from one unit to a new one, a case of robbing Peter to pay Paul. The 116th was to be at full strength, equipped, trained, and ready to go overseas 77 days after activation. It would be, however, over a year before the company deployed overseas, and over two years before it saw action in Europe.[74]

The 116th was not the only radio intelligence unit created or formed during the buildup. Cadres for the 113th, 114th, and 115th Radio Intelligence Companies arrived at Camp Crowder in June 1942. Nor was the 116th immune from providing personnel to serve as cadre for other units. In 1943 the company provided the cadre for the 34th Signal Construction Battalion.[75]

From May to October 1942, the 116th assisted in the building of Camp Crowder, conducted refresher basic training, and pulled a fair share of post police details. In June a typical day consisted of calisthenics in the morning, an hour's drill, and then fatigue details for the remainder of the day. In July some of the personnel were able to begin attending code school. In October the last large group of personnel arrived for the 116th and basic training began all over again.[76]

Refresher basic training consisted of classes in first aid, map reading, military courtesy, and many other subjects. Every Friday the unit stood inspection. Each soldier's weapon had to be cleaned, the walls and floors scrubbed, and windows washed before a pass would be issued. Basic training culminated in a week long bivouac, a test of endurance and basic book learning.

Of the 250 men who started the bivouac, only 84 completed the entire week of training.[77]

After the unit finished their basic training, the men attended the Midwestern Signal Corps School to learn morse code. Their goal was 25 words per minute with a typewriter. Those who dropped out early usually wound up becoming the unit's cooks, mechanics, drivers, wire men, etc. After completing the code school in the spring of 1943, the unit established its own code school to maintain the skills gained. During a pass in review, Major General Ben Lear, the Second US Army commander, remarked that the 116th was the best looking unit on the parade field. The soldiers consoled themselves saying, "Even if we can't do anything else, we can sure parade."[78] In May 1943, the 116th finally left Camp Crowder for Fort Du Pont in Delaware.[79]

The 114th Radio Intelligence Company was activated at Camp Crowder, Missouri, on 13 July 1942. The initial group of personnel stayed with the 116th until their barracks area could be completed. The company received basic training as a unit after the men arrived from the induction center in late October 1942. Those soldiers who were to be trained as intercept operators attended the 13 week school to learn basic morse code. After code training, they returned to their unit. It then became a unit responsibility to train its personnel in radio intelligence work. Classes conducted by the 114th consisted of receiver, transmitter, and antenna familiarization; code maintenance; and intercept operations.[80]

The problems with training of radio intelligence units became noticeable during the 1943 summer maneuvers. One observer to the Second Army's maneuver in Tennessee felt the 113th Radio Intelligence Company was very well trained while the opposing company, the 114th, was not. Both units formed and trained at Camp Crowder. The rationale given for the state of the 114th's training was the poor quality of personnel.[81] The 129th and 118th Signal Radio Intelligence Companies participated in the next series of Second Army maneuvers. From the observer's comments, both units appeared to be well trained and attempted to follow the doctrinal employment outlined in FM 11-20.[82]

Radio intelligence units came under the control of the Signal Intelligence Division, Office of the Chief Signal Officer, for training purposes upon their arrival in the European Theater of Operations (ETO). The purpose of the training was to familiarize intercept and direction finding operators with the type of traffic they would encounter on the continent. This training took between two and four months to complete.[83]

The training began by teaching operators how to recognize German signals. The requirement for intercept operators was to identify the country of origin within 30 seconds after signal acquisition. Then the operators learned the tactical traffic they were to intercept. Initially, the instructors used simulated German radio nets to teach techniques and procedures. After demonstrating proficiency, the operators copied, under close instructor supervision, assigned specific German transmitters. The instructors corrected any errors made and assessed the operators' state of training. This training in England gave most radio intercept and direction finding operators their first taste of actual intercept operations. After completion of the training cycle, the radio intelligence unit was normally assigned to an army or army group.[84]

A typical training intercept operation in the United Kingdom had approximately 20 receivers in one room. The companies rotated in four shifts to maximize both personnel training and intercept volume. The intercept operators usually copied in pencil, because they found they had to keep one hand free to "coax" the receiver. Equipment, both German and American, tended to wander off the dialed frequency. Operators discovered that the speed of German transmissions rarely exceeded 15 words per minute.[85]

While in England, administrative and tactical control of a radio intelligence company rested with the army or army group to which it was assigned. The "trick chief" (noncommissioned officer in charge of the intercept shift) had some means of communication with the intelligence personnel. The intelligence personnel provided the tactical direction and nominated targets for the radio targets to intercept. Normally the enemy units targeted were at army level or below, with the principle effort at division level. The main purpose of setting up the radio intelligence companies in England was to begin developing a order of battle database on the German units they could expect to face once the invasion began.[86]

While training in England, the signal intelligence units could intercept intelligence information that became of some value later in the war. For example, in April 1944, the 118th Radio Intelligence Company began intercepting German traffic for practice. Their copy revealed German troop movements to and along the Atlantic Wall. The intercept also showed certain radio characteristics (call signs, types of codes used, etc.) which were later used in identifying and locating German units in the field.[87]

After their arrival in England, the 114th spent approximately two weeks in conditioning their men before placing their intercept and direction finding personnel in the SIS training. After completing the course, they established procedures to conduct a controlled intercept mission. It became a practice within the company to interchange intercept and direction finding operators so they could gain a better appreciation of one another's job.[88]

Training of the newly created corps level signal service companies presented a new problem. Some, like the 3250th, had already been trained as the radio intelligence platoon of the 29th Division. Others, like the 3254th, had to begin their training program from scratch and rely on transfers from other units to provide the initial expertise.

The origin of the 3250th can be traced to the 29th Signal Company's radio intelligence platoon in late 1942. The division and the company deployed from the United States to England in October 1942. Little intelligence work was done as the division conducted basic training for the last three months of the year. However, the radio intelligence platoon managed to get five operators trained by sending them to the 121st Radio Intelligence Company for temporary duty. Upon their return, they began training other operators within the company. In January 1943, the platoon set up a small intercept station, mainly directed towards raising code speed and training in procedure and types of traffic used by the Germans. The training suffered a setback when three of their five trained operators were transferred from the radio intelligence platoon to radio operations section of the signal company. They received replacements from Camp Crowder, but the state of their training was low.[89]

The platoon made contact with SIS in London and arranged for a courier between the two sites. The platoon provided SIS with copies of the traffic it intercepted, logs, and summary reports. This arrangement provided the platoon with firsthand, low threat training, giving it an opportunity to fix and refine its procedures and improve the skills of its personnel. The 3250th was formally activated on 14 April 1944. From activation until its arrival in France, the 3250th participated in landing exercises, trained drivers in convoy movements, waterproofed equipment, prepared for the invasion of the continent, and conducted collection operations whenever possible.[90]

The route taken by the 3254th is completely different from that of the 3250th. The 3254th activation occurred five days after the 3250th's, 19 April 1944, but it did not have the luxury of already existing as a unit prior to activation. The personnel from the 3254th came from the 50th Signal Battalion initially, with additional teams and personnel coming from army level signal radio intelligence companies already in theater. By 9 June the company finally came together as a whole, just seven weeks after activation and four weeks after receipt of the alert order for overseas movement.[91]

The training program established by the 3254th for the few weeks it remained in England concentrated on non-radio intelligence skills. The program was eight weeks long, and consisted of classes in teletype operation, message center procedure, and switchboard installation and operation. They sent their intercept and direction finding operators on temporary duty to the 114th, 121st, and 137th Radio Intelligence Companies to gain experience on the German target.[92] For the majority of these operators, it would be refresher training, since they had just left similar units.

The radio intelligence units had specific comments about training received prior to D-day. In the spring of 1944, the Office of the Chief Signal Officer, Army Ground Forces, War Department, sent a questionnaire to radio intelligence units asking about equipment, tables of organization, training, and operations. Overall, commanders of the radio intelligence companies felt the training they received prior to arrival in the theater was inadequate. Too much time was spent on tactical training, too much "spit and polish," not enough time was spent on technical training.[93]

Doctrine and Organization - German Forces

Before the war, Germany had three types of signal intelligence units. Static radio intercept stations had been in existence since the 1920s. Radio intercept companies were attached to the army level signal battalions. Divisions had radio intercept platoons as authorized by the Versailles Treaty (see chapter 1). Knowledge they gained from the Russian and North African fronts early in the war led the Germans to centralize their intercept operations to increase efficiency. By fall 1942, short range signal intelligence companies, composed of the divisions' intercept platoons were formed and attached to the army level signal regiments. In 1943 the Germans formed signal intelligence battalions and regiments."

Based on further experience and tests in 1944, the Germans further expanded the short-range signal intelligence units by forming signal intelligence teams to support a division. They also formed corps evaluation units to control and guide these teams and perform rudimentary cryptanalysis on low grade enciphered traffic.[94]

At the army group level, a signal reconnaissance

regiment *(Nachrichtenaufklaegsrungsregiment)* was attached under the command of the signal officer. These regiments generally consisted of two battalions, each battalion having one long range signal intelligence company *(Fernaufklaerungskompanie)* and one or two short range signal intelligence companies *(Nahaufklaerungskompanien)*. The number of short range companies varied between battalions. The army group attached short range companies to subordinate armies, which then subattached platoons down to subordinate corps. The long range company remained under regimental control, intercepting strategic level traffic, while the other units collected operational and tactical intelligence that had immediate use to a maneuver commander.[96]

Monitoring the Allied build-up to establish the center of troop concentrations and movement in Great Britain became the main mission of the long range reconnaissance companies in the west. After the Normandy invasion began, the long range units continued to monitor the British Isles and then shifted their focus to monitoring Allied traffic along the French coast. Short range units, on the other hand, concentrated on units in contact with German forces, focusing mainly on artillery and armored unit nets.[97]

This emphasis on collecting tactical material

necessitated unique methods of dissemination. Security meant little to the Germans if it prevented a ground commander from receiving timely warnings of impending Allied, attacks or bombings. If an urgent clear text message was intercepted, the division's signal intelligence team immediately provided the information to its G-2 and corps evaluation unit simultaneously. Messages, whether transmitted in the clear or encoded, intercepted by the long or short range companies were sent to their battalion's evaluation center. If the message could not be solved at this level, it was sent to the regiment's evaluation center. A broadcast transmitter at evaluation centers sped the reporting process. At army group and lower levels, a radio set was dedicated to this broadcast channel. If a specific German unit was mentioned in an Allied message, that unit would be notified through the broadcast, usually within two hours after intercept. Other urgent messages sent through the broadcast included those identifying bombing and artillery targets, Allied troop movements and locations close to German lines, and any report revealing knowledge of German maneuver plans.[98]

The Germans concentrated their signal intelligence efforts to obtain information from which they could gain quick and operationally useful results. They did not establish a network to obtain material comparable to Allied ULTRA intercepts. For example, in 1944 coverage of the Washington-Algiers and Southern England-Algiers links was dropped after a few days because no messages were passed in the clear. The Germans did have some success breaking into higher echelon traffic, but their effort paled compared to the Allies.[99]

CHAPTER THREE - WARTIME OPERATIONS

A message intercepted in Italy at 1525A, 26 January 1944 reported: "Heavy vehicular traffic in both directions on S. VITTORE CERVARO road. Route is completely packed. Worthwhile target for artillery."[100]

Action taken: message relayed to corps artillery, which warned its flash and sound battalions to be on the alert for German artillery batteries capable of firing on this road. American artillery fired on the German gun positions with a minimum of delay after the Germans began firing. The 36th Division sent MPs to the traffic block, and the corps traffic control section took steps to improve traffic control along the road.[101]

Another intercepted message, this time at 1633A on 27 January 1944 reported:

K-8 occupied by enemy. The 11 Co which was put in is reduced to 10 men. Tank attack. 9 Co is 250 meters N of Hill 389. Heavy losses. I intend to attack at 1800 with the 10 Co from Hill 290 to the 9 Co on Hill 389 and assume the defensive on this line. Urgently request arty fire on Hill 389 and on high ridge W of Hill 290. According to PW statement enemy strengths at Hills 290 and 389 is 2 battalions. Request immediate answer. Signed: ZELLNER. [102]

This action took place in the sector of the French Corps in Italy. Americans warned their G-2 about the message as soon as it was received. What might have been a dangerous German counterattack against the exposed French flank instead turned into a German defeat. The II Battalion, 134th Infantry Regiment was nearly wiped out, and the French took over 100 prisoners of war.[103]

The two messages above provide an indication of the immediate feedback a radio intelligence unit could provide to a commander. But the importance of radio intelligence laid in the mundane, rountine, day to day operations. The capabilities of radio intelligence units, as a combat intelligence agency, were identification of enemy units, location of enemy units, movements of enemy units, and enemy intentions.[104] In other words, the bulk of intercept supported the development of order of battle databases, providing enemy unit information and locations to the G-2 team for incorporation with other intelligence into a report.

The Signal Intelligence Division, Office of the Chief Signal Officer (OCSigO), ETOUSA, handled the signal intelligence activities of the First US Army Group (later to be redesignated as Twelfth Army Group) until late December

1943. These activities included obtaining approval of T/O&Es for the Army Group Signal Intelligence Service, the signal intelligence service organization for the corps, and establishing combined signal intelligence and Y Service (the British radio intelligence organization) policies.[105] As mentioned in the previous chapter, OCSigO, ETOUSA also controlled the training of arriving radio intelligence units until their assignment to an army or corps.

Two signal intelligence units, the 114th and 116th Radio Intelligence Companies, remained under 12th Army Group control throughout the war. Others, as they entered the theater, would work at the group level before going to their assigned army or corps. Organizationally, the 3146th Signal Service Group provided direct control over their operations, as well as all other signal units belonging to the 12th Army Group. By May 1945, a signal service battalion, the 3906th would control all radio intelligence units.[106]

The radio intelligence company at the army level generally was twice the size of the corps units. Under T/O 11-77, dated 1 April 1942, the company had a total strength of 259; 8 officers and 251 enlisted men.[107] Besides conducting its own intercept and direction finding operations, the army radio intelligence company coordinated the work among the subordinate corps units. There were few major differences in operational procedures between corps and army level units.

Intercept Operations

The normal army level radio intercept section consisted of the operations officer, a warrant officer, and four intercept sections (tricks) of 25 men each.[108] Each trick had a noncommissioned officer in charge, known as the "trick chief," and a varying amount of operators manning intercept positions depending on the traffic level, time, and current situation. The trick chief controlled the collection, checked frequencies, and acted as a liaison between the radio operators and the traffic analysis section. The average working day within Third Army's RI units had tricks manning eight intercept positions from 0001-0800 and fifteen intercept positions from 0800-1600 and 1600-2400 hours. The trick not on duty for the day normally pulled the guard and other fatigue details that day.[109]

Other units modified procedures to suit their needs. For example, the 3250th manned five, twelve, and twelve positions for their three shifts. Observing that the majority of their intercept came during daylight hours, the 3250th determined that asymetrical manning made better use of their personnel. This allowed each operator to have one day off every seven or eight days, thus reducing burnout.[110]

To ensure good copy of key message the trick chief could assign two operators to cover the same traffic. This was referred to as "double banking." During times of heavy radio activity, the trick chief might assign two radio operators to conduct random search operations. These operators scanned the frequency spectrum until they heard an enemy net. They then passed the call signs and frequency to another operator to copy the message, while they resumed their search mission.[111]

Although originally organized similiarly, after deployment each corps' signal service company developed its own unique organization and methods of operation. The signal service companies were organized from existing resources in theater to provide SIGINT support to corps. Each new company had their own analytic personnel as part of its table of organization. This differed from the army's radio intelligence companies, which had analysts attached from the SIS. Another difference between the army and corps units was the need to copy German voice traffic. The close proximity of corps units to the front required operators to copy German voice traffic. Voice traffic was low in volume, and often did not carry much of tactical intelligence importance to the corps. In the 3255th Company, voice collection operators came from the intercept section, while in the 3256th they came from the analysis section.[112]

Direction Finding Operations,

Generally, each company had two or three direction finding teams, depending on the situation. The size of the army's radio intelligence company allowed it to operate three direction finding outstations. Baseline lengths ranged from 40 miles when controlled with wire to 60 miles with radio control. One DF team always colocated with the company's intercept section. This ensured an azimuth would be provided for traffic analysts to use in their reports.[113]

Wire remained a constant problem for RI units. Use of wire limited the length of a direction finding baseline. Wire also could be cut and interrupt DF operations. RI units had to keep wire teams available to lay, recover, and repair wire to the outstations. The 3250th's company log noted that, on 27 July 1944, they had to replace one half mile of wire chewed up by British tanks.[114] In August the company laid 143 miles of wire and the company was not even authorized a wire team.[115]

Units used differing methods to control direction finding operations. The 3253rd placed a DF person in the intercept trucks to act as liaison between the intercept and DF sections. The 3254th used an intercept operator to "pipe" signals to the colocated DF station, which then relayed it to the other outlying stations.[1'-6]

Within the 3250th the TA section supervised the control of direction finding. The best method was "direct" wire control, but the time and amount of wire needed to set up the net was too extensive to be practical. The company modified the procedure by laying wire from the DF team to the nearest telephone, thus reducing the amount of time and wire needed. This allowed the company to call the DF outstations through the regular army telephone system. A drawback to the "indirect" was lack of control over the intermediate wire and switches. Any problem along the line interfered with assigning missions and obtaining DF results. In February 1945, with the more sensitive DF sets, the company decided to try the direct method again, this time using radios. Modeled after the procedures used by the 113th RI Company, this system had the advantage of being more flexible and rapid than using telephone.[117]

Direction finding had many problems throughout the war. Outmoded equipment and a reliance on wire to pass instructions stand out as the two major problems faced by units. In Normandy the 3254th's DF team operated with fair results as long as their positions were close to the enemy. But after the breakout, the DF team had difficultly keeping up with the rapid pursuit pace set by the combat units.[118] The equipment used during this period was the SCR-503, a man portable piece of equipment that weighed over 600 pounds.[119] Finally, the 3254th secured new equipment, a SCR-555 modified with an improved antenna loop. With the use of improved equipment and combined outstations, DF became more productive in support of VIII Corps.[120]

The 3250th operated a maximum of three direction finders at any one time during their operations on the continent. Initially the company located the DF teams based on terrain and propagation considerations, but they found this did not provide adequate security for the men and equipment. In late August 1944 they began placing the teams with other troops, usually with a divisional signal company. In some instances DF teams might be placed with adjacent corps for a short time.[121]

The first DF set used by the 3250th was the SCR-503, which the unit found to have poor sensitivity. Later they used the SCR-206, which they modified by twisting wire around the DF loop antennas to increase the sensitivity.

In December 1944 the FUSA SIS detachment issued them a German direction finder, the TP(LM) 6/315.

Comparison tests by the company showed the German DF set had greater sensitivity than American DF equipment. By February the 3250th used three DF sets, two German and one British in their operations.[122]

Despite the problems, the units overcame the obstacles. Third Army's SIS detachment remarked that direction finding results from the signal services companies were uniformly good during the Battle of the Bulge, the clearing of the Saar-Moselle triangle, and the battle of the Rhine.[123]

Traffic Analysis

Units commonly divided the traffic analysis section into two main groups: traffic analysis and cryptanalysis departments. The section had four basic functions:

- Analysis and processing of traffic/identification of enemy radio nets;

- Cryptanalysis of low grade enemy ciphers;

- Determination of German order of battle (OB) and maintaining files on units, personalities, code names, and other necessary data; and,

- Compilation of statistics on technical aspects to aid in identification and analysis of traffic.[124]

The TA platoon also plotted the DF bearings from its

outstations. Whenever possible one person tasked the outstations and acted as a DF analyst. He maintained an overlay of enemy locations; previous day's bearing's, cuts, and fixes; and other pertinent information. If the unit obtained a large number of bearings on a specific enemy unit, a special overlay could be made charting that unit's movements.[125]

The traffic analysis platoon also prepared a daily report that went to higher and adjacent units. The report contained items dealing with:

- Intelligence Summary (brief);
- Decoded messages and Translations;
- Technical Summary of Nets Heard;
- Message Count/Set Allocation [tasking];
- Direction Finding Bearings; and,
- Code Identifications and Cipher Keys.[126]

At the army level, they found it necessary to establish a special section within the TA section to conduct coordination among corps, flanking armies, and higher SIS sections. Information traveled up and down this channel, sharing technical information concerning codes and ciphers, patterns of traffic, and other non-tactical information dealing with the enemy. The cryptanalytic section at army was larger than at corps. Third Army established teletype links between the corps' service companies and the 118th RI Company to pass low grade encrypted traffic for the army RI unit to break. This was often faster than trying to have the corps try to decipher traffic; it allowed the corps units to concentrate on intercept and DF operations. The army RI company could interpret intelligence on a wider basis, since it had data flowing in from several units. The 118th could coordinate radio intelligence matters with 12th Army Group or even SIS, ETOUSA.[127]

The 3250th TA section maintained liaison with the V Corps G-2 and the 113th RI Company at First Army through direct phone links and daily visits. They provided their daily report to the G-2 in the morning and a review of the day's events in the evening. Anything of immediate tactical value was sent to the G-2 at once. All results from traffic analysis, cryptanalysis, and DF were fused with known OB data and provided to the G-2 for inclusion in his daily activity report.[128]

In return, the V Corps G-2 provided every piece of enemy radio equipment and any captured documents pertaining to radio, codes, ciphers, call signs, or frequencies to the RI officer for examination. The radio intelligence unit also interviewed signal prisoners of war to gain additional insight into enemy communications procedures.[129]

Monitoring Allied Nets

The monitoring of friendly nets within Third Army began within twenty four hours after becoming operational. It had a dual purpose: monitor units for security violations, and correct net and radio procedures. The resources for the mission were not available, nor did any RI unit receive training for this mission. Within First and Third Armies, the RI companies made four receivers and operators available for the monitoring mission. The subordinate corps' companies had to make two receivers with operators available for this mission within their own units.[130]

Generally, Third Army assigned these missions for three to five days. The units reported serious violations immediately by phone or direct teletype to the Signal Intelligence Service, which in turn notified the unit concerned. Later, special units (Signal Information and Monitoring (SIAM) Companies) would be established to perform this function,[131] but the mission would never be totally removed from the radio intelligence or signal service company's inventory until after V-E Day.[132] A detachment from the 3103rd Signal Service Battalion was attached to the 3250th in January 1945 to do the friendly monitoring work.[133]

Unit Case Studies

3250th Signal Service Company (RI)

The V Corps activated its provisional Signal Radio Intelligence Company on the 14th of March, 1944 at Brockley Camp, near Bristol, England. Personnel came from many other signal units. The old radio intelligence platoon from the 29th Infantry Division formed the core of the company. Personnel also came from the 118th and 124th RI Companies, the 56th Signal Battalion, and other sources to fill the table of organization. On 14 April, the company officially became the 3250th Signal Service Company (RI). By the first of May, it had almost reached full strength.[134]

The company had little time to prepare itself for the upcoming invasion. In less than six weeks they formed and organized a corps radio intelligence company with only 25 percent of the enlisted men and one officer trained in intercept work. They drew 100 percent of their equipment, distributed it among the various sections, trained their people in the nomenclature, maintenance, and use of their equipment, and conducted operational intercept missions for almost a month. They also waterproofed their vehicles, participated in FABIUS I, the practice landing exercise for the invasion of Normandy, and trained in motor convoy movements. By 14 May the company began preparing for their movement into France.[135]

Prior to D-Day, the company divided itself into two operational detachments. The operational detachment, Detachment A, contained a complete functional radio intelligence section, with 5 officers and 75 men. Detachment B had the rest of the company, consisting of 3 officers and 50 soldiers. The company also had to provide a small detachment, or marching party, to go aboard the USS ANCON, the headquarters ship for V Corps. This party came from Detachment A. The mission of the marching party was to monitor V Corps radio nets for radio silence and later pass information collected from front line units to the corps headquarters.[136]

Detachment A embarked on board Landing Ship Tank (LST) 134 on 3 June, set sail on 5 June, and arrived off the coast of Normandy on the morning of 6 June. The invasion planners initially scheduled the 3250th Signal Service Company to land on the beach at H+950 minutes (almost 16 hours after the invasion began) in the first wave of the second tide after the invasion began. This would have put them on the beach around 2200 on 6 June. Instead they ended up spending the night of D-Day aboard ship under enemy air raids. They finally began disembarking in three groups at 1700 on D+1, almost 19 hours after their original landing time.[137]

The first group landed without experiencing any problems and proceeded to the vehicle transit area. The corps headquarters directed the company to establish its first site within 100 yards of the corps command post. This site was within one half mile of enemy lines and came under sniper fire.[138]

The second group's landing did not go as smoothly as the first group's. Their landing craft struck a sandbar about 150 yards from shore and they were told to drive to shore. One truck hit a shell hole about five yards from shore and required a tractor to pull it to shore. The radio truck's motor died short of shore, but another truck pulled it to shore. The wire truck stalled halfway to shore, forcing the men to swim the rest of the way. A DF truck sank after leaving the landing craft. The men saved some of the equipment floating around them, loaded it onto another ferry, and never saw it gain. The second group, soggy and missing two trucks, finally joined the first group the next morning.[139]

The third group left the LST at 2100 hours. By 2200 they had grounded, but could not land, as their boat was directly over a submerged mine field. Forced to reverse and try again, they grounded on another sandbar at 2215. They refused to disembark based on their judgment of the depth of the surrounding water, having observed the sunken boats nearby. The group finally landed on the beach by 2230, rejoining the company that night.[140]

The marching party loaded on the USS ANCON on 24 May and trained for their mission until they set sail. Their convoy left England on the fifth of June, arriving off the French coast around midnight. The detachment began monitoring the V Corps radio nets to enforce radio silence prior to the landings. At 0630 on the sixth, they began monitoring traffic from the 1st and 29th Infantry Divisions, and provided the corps headquarters information on the progress of the assault. This mission continued until late on 7 June, when they were released to rejoin the company.[141]

Detachment B consisted of the personnel, motor, mess, and supply sections, and portions of the radio repair, intercept, message center, radio, and direction finding sections. The detachment embarked on board the USS CLARA BARTON on 12 June and disembarked on 17 June, joining the forward detachment near Bernesq.[142]

In its after action report, V Corps praised the efforts of the 3250th. The company provided accurate information of enemy units, their strength, order of battle, and intentions. It also provided information on the progress of Allied units from enemy sources (reconnaissance patrol nets) which was faster than status reports through normal channels. The report goes on further to state that:

> ...on numerous occasions, units of V Corps were able to advance with a minimum of resistance by knowing in advance enemy intentions and dispositions. In Normandy, by close liaison with the Corps Artillery, it was possible to eliminate a number of enemy artillery observers. When the breaking out from the Normandy Beachhead was in progress, the company was able to give advance notice of the German intention to split the First and Third Armies at MORTAIN, France. Before the SIEGFRIED Line, in October, the movement of a German Panzer division to the Corps front was reported well in advance. On the occasion of the German "ARDENNES" offensive, the up to the minute location, movement, and intentions of the northern German spearhead was reported.[143]

114th Signal Radio Intelligence Company

The 114th RI Company arrived in France to support 12th Army Group on 17 August 1944, two years and one month after its activation at Camp Crowder.[144] Unfortunately, little of the company's operational records survived, being destroyed due to the secrecy of the work. The report files by the 114th are mostly of a technical nature, with little operational information.[145]

The 114th did try the leapfrog method of moving, but felt it did not work for them. The requirement for a messenger service between the forward and rear sites and additional wire circuits exceeded the benefits gained. Instead, the 114th could tear down operations in an hour, move to the new site, and reinstall equipment to resume the mission 90 minutes after arriving at the new location. Including travel time, the company accomplished its movement generally within 18 hours.[146]

The amount of traffic intercepted by the 114th ranged between 6,000 to 7,000 messages per month.[147] Between June 1944 and V-E Day, the 114th intercepted about 55,000 messages. From its arrival on the continent to the end of the war, it provided over 7,750 items of locational information obtained through direction finding operations (summarized in Table 1). The totals for October, November, and December, when the front was relatively static, are much higher than the other months. This indicates that DF could provide a great deal of locational information if the outstations had time to establish themselves and lay wire to their control. The times when the unit displaced forward more often (August-September and January through May) show the difficulty of establishing a baseline that relied on wire for its tasking and reporting.[148]

	Bearings	Cuts	Fixes	Total
August	118	0	0	118
September	658	94	0	752
October	1,259	137	3	1,399
November	1,109	174	25	1,308
December	726	227	59	1,012
January	456	242	68	766
February	572	221	119	912
March	794	328	169	1,291
April	204	19	8	231
Total	5,896	1,442	451	7,789

Table 1. Direction finding results for 114th Signal Radio Intelligence Company - August 1944 to April 1945.

113th Signal Radio Intelligence Company

The Army activated the 113th at Camp Crowder on 15 June 1942, with the initial cadre coming from the 125th RI Company. In 1943 the company went on maneuvers with the 81st Infantry Division. After the exercise the company was assigned to the Eastern Defense Command and moved to Hollywood, Florida, to carry out missions assigned by the Office of the Chief Signal Officer, Washington, D.C. There the unit established an intercept station and installed a 310 mile direction finding baseline. After completing the assigned missions, the 113th went to the United Kingdom, arriving on 16 December 1943.[149]

While in England, the unit's operators underwent training by SSD ETOUSA on German army procedures. In the United States they had concentrated their training on high speed commercial and special German diplomatic traffic. This proved useless in the operational and tactical environment in Europe. After completing the SSD training, they moved near Colyton, Devonshire, and established an intercept site at Beer Head. Here the company intercepted medium and low grade German traffic. The British Army provided an experienced sergeant to assist the operators. On 8 June they dismantled the site, and arrived in Normandy on 13 June to support First US Army.[150] For the first few weeks in France, the company worked out the "bugs" in their systems and procedures.

Since they copied the German radio traffic by hand, there was no need for typewriters in their intercept shelters. They also found they did not use the recorders. They removed the equipment to make more room for control and intercept personnel in the shelters.[151]

The 113th also modified doctrinal procedures for

conducting DF operations. Initially they used wire to control the DF baseline as outlined in the FM. However, during the rapid movement across France after the breakout, they found wire could not keep up with the DF sections. Their wire teams worked as long as 19 hours a day after the St. Lo breakthrough because of the extensive requirements for DF. They then began using radio to control the baseline and to collect the data from the sections.[152]

Observations

The Third Army's SIS detachment made the following observations after the war concerning radio intelligence activities:

a. Training of operators, particularity in voice interception, was inadequate. Many of the attempts at VHF interception failed to poor language skills as well as to equipment problems. The army had not considered voice interception to be a primary function of signal intelligence units. The majority of the military communications worldwide prior to the war relied on continuous wave and morse code. VHF radio had just begun to be fielded and was not in widespread military use. It was futile to take intercept radio operators trained in morse code and expect them to understand the intricacies of foreign military jargon.[153]

b. Direction finding equipment was not suitable, especially for fast paced operations. The direction finding equipment worked well enough, but it could have been better. The equipment fielded was not mobile enough, especially at the corps level where they were much closer to the front. Receiver sensitivity was also a problem.[154]

c. The wire teams at corps signal units were inadequate and inhibited operations. A wire team was needed at both corps and army level to maintain the lines from the control section to the DF teams. However, lack of a wire team actually improved the responsiveness of DF operations. Some units solved the problem by using radio to control the DF operation. Though new procedures had to be developed, nonauthorized equipment gained, and additional ciphers created, the use of radio allowed for faster tasking and return of bearings. This, in turn, provided the analysts a better opportunity to identify and locate German units.[155]

CHAPTER FOUR - INTELLIGENCE OPERATIONS

As mentioned in the previous chapter, American units conducted radio intercept operations prior to their arrival on the continent. During the six weeks prior to the invasion, RI units intercepted practice traffic, which also provided order of battle intelligence. The units developed data on unique radio characteristics that would assist them in identifying German units and analyzing messages.[156]

The two case histories discussed below provide a snapshot of intercept collection results from army and corps level radio intelligence units. Unfortunately, most RI units destroyed their operational records after the war, mainly because of the secrecy involved in their work, but also to reduce their baggage for the trip home.

Third United States Army

Prior to its activation on 1 August 1944, the Third US Army's radio intelligence companies were already operating in France. On 15 July the 118th Signal Radio Intelligence Company arrived in France and began operations. The 3254th Signal Service Company arrived on 29 June and supported VIII Corps headquarters.[157]

The bulk of intelligence intercept came from German armored forces, the Panzer (Pz) and Panzergrenadier (PzGndr) divisions. The major units TUSA radio intelligence units followed were the Panzer Lehr, 11th Pz, 2d Pz, and the 17th SS PzGndr divisions. TUSA units also intercepted the 2d SS Pz, 9th SS Pz, 10th SS Pz, 21st Pz, 3rd PzGndr, 15th PzGndr, 265th Infantry, 266th Infantry, 272d Infantry, 348th Infantry, and 553rd Infantry divisions, just to name a few.

On D-Day reconnaissance traffic from the 21st Pz Division indicated that the unit was committed in the Caen sector. Other intelligence gleaned before the breakout indicated that the 2d SS Pz Division *(Das Reich)* had no shortage of ammunition. After the combined VII and VIII Corps breakout attack on 27 July, intercept from German reconnaissance units provided American forces with a detailed description of Allied gains. Intercepts on the 31st of July and 1st of August revealed a need for artillery ammunition in the 2d SS Pz Division. It was also determined that the division's headquarters were located at Montbray. Five days later the 2d SS Pz Division fell back to Le Menil Toye and began radio coordination with 2d Pz.[158]

As the Falaise pocket began to develop in August, radio intelligence identified that the majority of the Panzer units were on the left flank of TUSA, instead of in the front. As the noose began to tighten, radio intelligence provided the first indications of eastward movement of units caught within the pocket. On 15 August direction finding results established movement of the Panzer Lehr's reconnaissance elements to the east. In fact, throughout August DF tracked the movement of the Panzer Lehr from Falaise-Argentan across the Seine River, north of Paris until it moved out of the Third Army's sector.[159]

For four days at the end of August, captured documents allowed TUSA units to read the 9th Pz Division's traffic. The 3254th, working directly for Third Army while VIII Corps was involved in the Brittany Peninsula, collected most of the intercept. Information gained from these intercepts were the locations of divisional supply headquarters, ammunition and fuel dumps, and division headquarters. Intercept also revealed the existence of various *Kampfgruppen* (combat group) and the temporary subordination of elements of the 48th Infantry Division to the 9th Pz.[160]

On 30 August intercept provided the first indications of German reinforcement to France from Italy. Direction finding located the 3rd PzGndr Division reconnaissance elements in the vicinity of Nancy. The 3rd PzGndr supplied many interesting nuggets of information for analysts to work on. As the 3rd moved into its positions, their reconnaissance elements reported the locations of neighboring units, their command posts, and their main line of resistance. On the 20th of September, traffic from the 3rd PzGndr gave the indications of an upcoming German counterattack near Pourncy.[161]

September saw intercept continue much the same as before. German units, pressed hard by Patton's advance continued to retreat eastward. This deprived them of the opportunity to use wire, thus they had to rely on radio to coordinate their forces. Radio intelligence identified additional unit command posts, highlighted planned counterattacks, and noted the Germans' escape gap near Nancy. The highpoint came late in the month. The 3254th intercepted a reconnaissance report announcing a planned counterattack by Battalion "Schneider" in the vicinity of Foret de Gremmercy early on the morning of the 29th. The next day, the intercepted reconnaissance reports stated the counterattack had been repulsed.[162]

In October came the first indications that the front was beginning to stabilize. Across the Third Army's front radio activity was low. The first part of November also reflected low radio activity along the Moselle front. This enemy communications activity appears to have been pretty much routine, with the analysts maintaining continuity on the German formations to their front. During November the TUSA units noticed movement of German units along their front. The 21st Pz began moving northward, Panzer Lehr had withdrawn from the area, and contact had been lost with the 3rd PzGndr Division.[163]

The lull in German radio activity, and therefore in radio intercept, can be attributed to three primary factors. First the Germans had withdrawn, for the most part, back into friendly soil. Here they utilized wire for the majority of their communications. Second, forward movement slowed and Allied attacks diminished as the logistical lifelines became longer. Finally, Hitler began planning his Ardennes counteroffensive, *Wacht am Rhine* (Watch on the Rhine). Orders to units were couriered and staff officers were forbidden to transmit anything regarding the operation over the radio. Hitler imposed strict radio silence over the entire counteroffensive operation.

After the German attack on 16 December, the focus of Third Army's intercept effort shifted northward. TUSA units intercepted the Panzer Lehr, 3rd PzGndr, and 5th Parachute (Pcht) divisions, and located them through direction finding efforts. The attack brought the Germans back onto the air again. For example, the 5th Pcht transmitted in the clear continually as they reported on progress made and the status of American counterattacks.[164]

The defeat of the German advance, and their subsequent withdrawal, helped the month of January to be one of the more productive ones from a radio intelligence standpoint. Five divisions, the 3rd PzGndr, Panzer Lehr, 2d SS Pz, 21 Pz, and 17th PzGndr, were identified and located through SIGINT. Prisoner of war reports had previously indicated that the 2d SS Pz *(Das Reich)* had been transferred to the Eastern front, but radio intercept located elements of the division and warned the advancing units.[165] As German units pulled back, analysis coupled with direction finding allowed TUSA to stay abreast of German army movements. The radio intelligence companies tracked the Panzer Lehr to Bitburg and the 11 Pz Division to Saarburg.[166]

The activity level began to drop once again towards the latter part of February. The Third Army SIS attributed this to the gradual disintegration of the German communications systems, and the introduction of hastily formed units with little or no radio equipment. The majority of usable intelligence came in fragments. Items reported in March included the reappearance of a railroad gun, the status of bridges across the Rhine River at Mainz, and the commitment of flak units in a artillery role vice one of air defense.[167]

In April radio intercept began picking up German units in contact with Soviet forces, as the two fronts converged. The analysts tracked these units closely as well since they had the capability of shifting towards the west. After the Battle of the

Bulge, the Allies learned not to take Hitler for granted.[168]

Of particular note was the interception of the "Bavarian Freedom Movement." As the Americans began closing in, a group of Germans began broadcasting from the Munich area. They provided many items of importance to the Allies and Germans in the American held sector. Some of these included surrender instructions to other forces, the location of obstacles along the autobahns and highways, where Japanese diplomats assembled prior to fleeing Germany, and news about Hitler's death. After the end of the war the Third Army's radio intelligence units focused mainly on monitoring the surrender nets and watching for illicit or illegal radio transmissions.[169]

3254th Signal Service Company

The 3254th supported VIII Corps for the most of the European campaigns. For one brief period, from mid-August to mid-September 1944, the company worked directly for Third Army while VIII Corps was involved in the clearing of the Brittany Peninsula. From 16 September to 4 October it was assigned to the Ninth US Army (NUSA). After 4 October, the 3254th reverted under VIII Corps control for the remainder of the war.[170]

Information collected in July consisted mostly of reconnaissance patrol and artillery activity within the 2d SS Pz

Division *(Das Reich)*. There were also a few reports detailing some German supply problems and depot locations. The little amount of radio intercept gained stemmed chiefly from the static nature of the fighting in July. The Americans were busy working their way through the hedgerows. The Germans could use wire to handle the majority of their communications requirements.[171]

In August VIII Corps, in conjunction with VII Corps, broke through at St. Lo. When VIII Corps began the siege of Brest, the 3254th began working directly for TUSA. Using captured cipher keys, the company decoded the majority of the 9th Pz Division's communications at the end of August. Intelligence gleaned from this source included command post locations, fuel and ammunition supply points, and proposed lines of resistance.[172]

The first half of September offered few intelligence highlights. After being assigned to the Ninth US Army on the 14th, the 3254th began picking up the 3rd PzGndr Division as it entered the area of operations. The company could easily track the movement of the 3rd PzGndr through the latter's reconnaissance patrol nets. The radio operators could follow the battle's progress around Nancy through the 3rd PzGndr. They intercepted reports on road status within the sector, locations of German and American units, and resupply

79

routes.[173]

In October VIII Corps moved into Belguim on a front extending from St. Vith in the north to the Belgian-Luxembourg border, then onto Arlon in the south. Here the 3254th rejoined the corps. Intercept activity across the corps front was extremely low. Most traffic intercepted consisted of patrol activity, as the major German headquarters again returned to landline communications when they were in their fixed fortifications. Activity remained low through November as well. But December 16th found the 3254th and the rest of VIII Corps directly in front of the German 5th and 6th Panzer Armies.[174]

Between the 1st and 16th of December it appeared that the Germans would remain behind their fortifications and wait for the inevitable Allied push. The 3254th had little indication of the impending attack through radio intercept. The Germans effectively employed radio security as they massed their forces. The company moved twice in the next ten days.[175]

The 3254th knew of Patton and the Third Army's arrival to relieve Bastogne from the 15th Parachute Regiment of the 5th Parachute Division. On the 25th they intercepted messages reporting American tanks moving north from Arlon. The next day, the messages were frantically appealing for help as the regiment had been badly mauled by elements of the US III

Corps.[176]

In January the VIII Corps and the rest of the Allied armies pushed the German forces out of the "bulge." Radio activity remained high throughout the month as the Germans withdrew from Belgium. Radio intercept highlights included reconnaissance patrols from the 3rd PzGndr again, which conveniently reported all their observations on the progress of the battle. The 3rd PzGndr also unknowingly provided information on proposed lines of resistance, command posts, and depot areas. On 30 January the company intercepted traffic from the 2d SS Pz Division *(Das Reich)* that indicated their movement to the Russian front.[177]

For the rest of the war radio intercept would provide Americans with the same type of intelligence described above. German forces were reeling under the American onslaught and had little time to establish secure wire communications. They were forced to rely on radios to coordinate their forces as best they could. Americans knew of impending counterattacks, which were then repulsed.

The 3254th provided a great deal of intelligence support to VIII Corps and TUSA. Appendix A contains a summary of intercept by type of traffic, the maximum positions manned, and the number of DF shots (bearings) per month. The short intelligence history written by the company indicates their operational focus was on identifying, locating, and tracking major German units.

German Intelligence

As brought forth in earlier chapters, the Americans and their allies were not the only ones practicing signal intelligence operations. The Germans realized the importance of SIGINT soon after the end of World War I. They understood that SIGINT could be a combat force multiplier, especially when the Versailles Treaty limited their armed forces to just 100,000 personnel.

A German prisoner of war, Oskar Bitzer of the 2d Company of the 256th Signal Battalion, 256th Infantry Division, stated the Americans were careless in their signal procedures, and that all regiments of the 79th US Infantry Division were identified through interception. Based on information gained from the messages, the Germans repelled an attack by the 79th in early December in the Hagenau Forest, north of Strasbourg. The Americans revealed the time and place of the attack, and the Germans took appropriate defensive countermeasures, movement of their troops and concentrating their artillery fire on the 79th Infantry Division.[178]

For the Germans, the most important source of intelligence came from signals intelligence. Most of their success came from intercepting low echelon traffic: armored and artillery nets passing operational traffic. Just as we exploited this level of communications, so too did the Germans capitalize on our mistakes. Artillery nets were given high priority. The Germans noticed that our call signs often remained the same for a unit over a significant period of time.[179]

The loss of German air reconnaissance forces led them to build up their signals intelligence effort in the west. Radio intelligence accounted for approximately 60 percent of all intelligence the Germans received on the western front.[180]

As stated before, the Germans utilized a broadcast net, or radio warning service, to disseminate intelligence information to subordinate units. To prevent the dissemination of radio intelligence to unauthorized parties, the Germans used three different cryptographic systems; one for army group and armies, one for corps, and the third for divisions.[181] The importance of this net cannot be overstated. For example, the Germans knew of the attack at St. Lo prior to its execution. On 18 July, Signal Battalion 13 reported that a new front line net had begun operations in the area surrounding St. Lo. Based on the reduction of artillery traffic in the north, and increased radio traffic in the south, the German Seventh Army G-2 deduced a major attack in vicinity of St. Lo would take place. The events of 25-26 July certainly bore out his prediction.[182]

Prior to the Allied invasion of France, the success of signal intelligence was limited. This was due mainly to secure Allied communications while in the United Kingdom. Yet a major focus of the German long range reconnaissance intercept battalions was coverage of tactical exercises. By monitoring a ground exercise in Great Britain in 1943, the Germans gained the following information:

a. The division's task was to destroy an enemy objective 20 kilometers inland from the beach.

b. The breath of the landing was 15 kilometers. Each brigade making the landing had a frontage of seven kilometers.

c. They knew the units participating in the exercise and their schedule for the three day battle.[183] The same team that intercepted this information also intercepted data concerning US Army maneuvers, exercises "Royal" and "Dry Run," and their locations.[184]

The G-2s of German units drew almost 60 percent of their intelligence from radio intercept after the invasion began. The other forty percent came from other sources, air reconnaissance, human reports, etc. As their retreat progressed from the Normandy beaches to the West Wall, signals intelligence came to play an ever increasing role.[185]

Signal Battalion 13 supported the Fifteenth Army. One

specific example of the intelligence they gained from American radios follows. On 13 June they intercepted an order for a bombing mission that targeted German infantry assembly positions and armored vehicles in a forest west of Giverville. They also intercepted orders for bombing missions against German infantry and armor at Courbeville, Sannerville, and Colombelles. The battalion broadcasted this intelligence to all divisions and corps within the German Fifteenth Army, especially those in which the troops concerned were mentioned. The information also was sent up their chain to the intelligence officer of the Fifteenth Army by both telephone and telegraph.[186]

An entry by the chief intelligence officer for the Fifteenth Army showed that this method worked well. He wrote:

> As a group, enemy messages intercepted by Western Theater Command and Signal Intelligence Battalion 13 allow an accurate estimate of the situation, especially in the combat zone west of the river Orne. Information on our movements is often more quickly obtained from intercepted messages than by our own reports.[187]

In the spring of 1944 German radio intelligence in France and Italy detected a shift in Allied concentrations away from the Mediterranean. One case showed an American airborne unit, possibly the 82nd Airborne Division, in southern Italy for quite a while, then it disappeared. A few weeks later intercept of an unidentified net in England allowed the Germans to relocate the unit prior to the invasion.[188]

An internal evaluation prepared after the Allied invasion showed that the Germans had identified approximately 95 percent of the units involved in the Normandy invasion while they were in the British Isles. Locator cards contained precise information on Allied units, their communication structure, and their involvement in exercises. However, the Germans did not get any indications of when the cross channel invasion would take place. The Allies achieved surprise on 6 June through the imposition of radio silence.[189]

General Albert Praun stated that the German communication intelligence organization had prepared for the Allied invasion. Technical data on Allied communications (ciphers, codes, call signs, etc.) had been distributed to all units. This made it possible to transfer coverage of units rapidly as only the updates to existing technical data base had to be transferred.[190]

The Allies mounted a deception operation, Operation "Fortitude," to cover the Normandy landings. The German high command believed that a second, the main, Allied landing would take place north around Calais. To defend against that possibility, the German reserves and the Fifteenth Army were not committed against the Normandy beachhead. Information gained from radio intercept did not support that conclusion. The chief of the control center of Communication Intelligence West believed Normandy was the main effort. A comparison of units identified on the beaches compared with those previously identified in England led to his conclusion.[191] Between D-Day and 25 June, communications intelligence had correctly identified the First US Army, four corps, and 15 divisions or parts of divisions. The order of battle correctly listed the 101st and 82nd Airborne, and the 90th Infantry Divisions under the control VIII Corps.[192]

The German radio intelligence structure had other successes. A few days after the invasion, the Allies created an impression of a second airborne landing by dropping parachute dummies. Radio intelligence determined this to be a ruse due to the lack of radio traffic from the supposed landing zone.[193] The breaking of a logistics code gave the Germans exact figures of men and materiel brought into the British Second Army bridgehead.[194]

Other results of radio intercept had a more immediate tactical impact. On 14 June, German radio reconnaissance intercepted traffic from the US XIX Corps that indicated they were moving and would attack the next day. They did, and the attack was halted by a stubborn German defense. Messages intercepted on an aerial reconnaissance net identified a major push in the Caen area.[195] On 16 March an Allied plane located a large concentration of German vehicles between Nonweiler and Eisen. The report giving the location and requesting air support was intercepted by the 256th Signal Battalion. They broadcast the information to the unit, which then moved to new cover before the air attack began.[196]

As the Germans withdrew to the West Wall, they could track the progress of Allied units through their communications. The Third US Army could easily be observed because messages were transmitted in a very careless manner. At the opposite end of the spectrum, the Seventh US Army was the most difficult for the Germans to observe. General Praun attributed this to the battle hardiness of the army from its time in North Africa and Sicily. The Seventh Army had trained its operators to such a high degree of radio discipline that any intelligence results were kept to a minimum.[197]

Once the lines were stabilized along the West Wall, the Germans transferred five radio intelligence companies from the eastern front to the west. These units provided an increase in long range intercept because of their experience against the Soviets. The additional collection assets allowed the Germans the opportunity to break American field ciphers quicker. Key targets were the daily status reports provided by headquarters to their superiors. Many units transmitted these reports at the same time every day, from the same station, in the same format. The regular, repetitive nature of the messages eased the solving of new ciphers soon after they were introduced. Collecting these messages also identified the Allied order of battle.[198]

German radio intelligence monitored Allied communications prior to the Ardennes counteroffensive. They observed that the Allies had no indications of the attack, or that German troops had massed. German radio intelligence units reported the American units holding the Ardennes had not fortified their positions. They also identified the fact there was no reserves immediately available for a counterattack.[199]

After the Germans launched their offensive, intercept provided information that may have changed the outcome had the Germans had the resources to exploit the situation. Shortly after the attack began, the Germans intercepted a new military police net in the First US Army zone. The Germans determined that MP units were positioned along two major north-south French highways, and that checkpoints had been established to facilitate the northward movement of American forces from the south. The Germans located 22 of the 35 checkpoints used by the Americans.

They also broke the cipher used by the MPs. The

information intercepted contained data on the composition of the units, their advance guards, speed of march, column lengths, time of departure and arrival, and number of vehicles. The radio intelligence unit estimated it intercepted almost 90 percent of the MP broadcasts and ascertained with almost 100 percent accuracy the units that had itineraries. This gave the German commander a complete picture of what was happening on his left flank, which allowed him to shift forces to sidestep the main thrust of the counterattack.[200]

German radio intelligence efforts focused on lower echelons where immediate results could be obtained. The ciphers and codes used by Allied tactical formations were often simple and easily broken by German cryptanalysts.

Bitzer, the German prisoner of war, told his interrogators that it was possible to decode two letter messages from the 3rd Cavalry Group within an hour. He also stated that the code names used for unit commanders were well known in the intercept business, and a manual for intercept operators containing this information had been published.[201]

Two other prisoners of war, from the Signal Intercept Team of the 18th Volksgrenadier Division, provided insights into the operation of German radio intelligence. According to them, a 1944 OKW order stated that one intercept team was to be assigned to each division. The team had a team leader, two interpreters with some signal knowledge and two to three radio operators. The team did not have any DF equipment, which they found to be a disadvantage. They kept a journal to record intercepted messages. Daily a list of the messages, plus copies of the message text, were sent to the KAST *(Korps Auswerte Staffel* (corps evaluation staff)).[202]

The KAST for 66 Corps directed that all two letter groups be reported immediately by phone, and that five letter group messages be recorded and delivered daily via courier at 1400. The KAST then passed the messages it could decipher to Signal Reconnaissance Battalion 13. The KAST also provided the teams with frequencies, call signs, and the possible unit identifications that were to be copied by the intercept teams.[203]

The team also searched the spectrum looking for additional frequencies and clear text messages. Until the end of November the only messages received in clear text came from an S-3 of a reconnaissance unit using code names "Brownie," "Dan," and "Smitty." They assumed these reports dealt with strength, but they did not know the content of the messages. The amount of messages intercepted prior to the beginning of the Ardennes offensive varied, but the team estimated an average of 20 per day was reasonable. Of these, 30 to 40 percent were uncoded messages.[204]

On the 16th of December the team found it impossible

to report intercepted two letter traffic. Communications links with the corps became very difficult due to the rapid movement of the German advance. The team did notice American security procedures became lax, most messages were sent in the clear. Some of the messages they remember intercepting were:

-Request permission to withdraw line Manderfeld-Andler.

-Position untenable, enemy armor NW and S of position.

-Destroy safe, bring back map 1:100,000.[205]

On 19 December, near St. Vith, the team intercepted messages concerning the fighting around the town; the positions of German armor, assault guns, and infantry; artillery reports; and requests for close air and artillery support. With German communications being weak, the team could provide their commander with reports of progress of their own troops as well.[206]

In summary, both prisoners of war were surprised at the relative long time between frequency changes and the number of repeated messages. The "say again" messages provided German interceptors additional opportunities to copy the message. They also noticed that when speed was essential, American radio operators often sent in the clear. They felt they were not hampered in their work by US security precautions or operating procedures, and that German radio traffic was more secure than American traffic.[207]

German Codes/Ciphers

Before the Allied invasion of France, the German communication system was fairly well fixed, using a known and systemic method of assigning call signs. With the aid of a captured call sign book, the Allies could easily identify intercepted nets and develop the order of battle. Radio intelligence units operating in England intercepted a great deal of coastal and slightly inland communications. These communications employed the medium and low grade traffic.[208]

The low grade enciphered traffic used the *Heeresignaltafel* (Army Signal list), or HST for short. The HST code was fairly well structured. It used a fixed list of 500 trigrams set against basic vocabulary that were suited to the needs of various units. The HST code could be changed periodically as the need arose.[209]

Other low grade German tactical codes used when the Allies invaded were the T/L and NI codes. These were used from division forward, and apparently were very easy to break. Many of the messages contained their unit locations, thus lessening the importance of direction finding.[210]

Some German units manning permanent fortifications

along the coast used another type of three letter code. This code employed many more trigrams than the HST code, and was changed monthly. This made it more secure than the HST code.[211]

After the invasion some of the codes began to disappear, particularly the one used by units along the coast. Noticed by intelligence units during the invasion was a propensity for German units to use a changing monoalphabetic system (one for one exchange) to encipher portions of a message. For example, the city of PARIS might be encoded as XUTSW in an otherwise clear text message. The use of this simple code became associated with certain units, particularly the 21st Panzer (Pz) Division.[212]

Early in June 1944 the Allies began receiving hints of a new German code called *Rasterschluessel.* In August they began intercepting random messages in this code. They also became aware of the enemy's intention to begin randomizing call sign selection as opposed to following a fixed and systematic method. Any change in call sign allocation or codes would make it more difficult to make unit identifications, establish net continuity, and track enemy movements.[213]

The changes in codes and call sign assignments meant the Allied traffic analysts had to work harder to identify a unit. Analytic procedures shifted towards identifying nets based on many pieces of scattered information. Known personalities and place names transmitted in the clear, types of codes used, no change in call signs, and signal security violations are just a few of the types of information an analyst used. Some of this information could be gained through interrogation of prisoners of war, especially signal troops. Other bits of the puzzle would fall in place only after long hours spent on intercept, recording, and analyzing patterns.[214]

The changes brought forth increased demands for more detailed records. Some of the files maintained by the analysts were personality files, unit composition and organization files, types of codes used, and historical DF information (to include composite data). All would be used to corroborate identifications.[215]

What type of code was used could sometimes identify the type of unit transmitting a signal. For example, German artillery employed simple letter substitution for numbers when passing map coordinates. The artillery for the 17th SS Panzergrenadier (PzGndr) Division *(Goetz von Berlichingen)* often used plain language inserts in their enciphered communications.[216]

Throughout the war the HST code was fairly common, with some units relying on it more than others. This also assisted the analyst in his job. The Panzer Lehr Division, 3rd Pz

Division, and the 116th Pz Division all used the HST with their own unique variant, thus producing easily identifiable unit characteristics. Surprisingly, German infantry divisions were unproductive for the most part from a radio intelligence standpoint. The reason given for this was their lack of mobility allowed them to rely on wire to a greater extent.[217]

Other codes intercepted by American radio intelligence units were a bigram code used by V-1 launching sites, a "Jargon" code consisting entirely of place names, and a simple transposition box used by the 2d Pz Division *(Das Reich)*. Together these codes, and the intelligence gained, made only a small portion of the intercept work. In the end, it would be the normal method of maintaining net continuity through intercept and DF that made radio intelligence work a valuable tool for the ground commander.[218]

Observations

The 3254th had three criticisms of operations in Europe. They believed corps level RI units should have been given medium grade cipher keys. Apparently the Army had a regulation prohibiting corps level units from using this material. Often there was a time lag of 24-28 hours from the intercept of medium grade messages to the message processing. The 3254th cited their work at the end of August as an example of the benefit of having corps level units process medium grade messages. The company also recommended a G-2 representative be trained to handle medium grade messages.[219]

The second criticism concerned the G-2. The unit felt that technical information was overlooked because no one at G-2 had signal intercept expertise. Technical information dealt with call signs, frequencies, cipher type, message and group lengths, and other characteristics used to identify an enemy unit. Many times an enemy unit, once a sufficient technical data base had been developed, was identified from technical charactertics without having to decipher the message. The recommendation that a signal intelligence officer be assigned or attached to the G-2 had merit as it would ensure someone in the G-2 possessed technical signal intercept knowledge. The duties would include liaising between the G-2 and the signal intercept unit; processing captured enemy signal documents that came into the corps; and identifying prisoners of war who might have knowledge of signals, communications, or intelligence techniques.[220]

The third recommendation dealt with the signal service company organization. The lack of a TO&E wire team meant the unit had to use intercept and DF operators to lay and recover wire between positions. Also noted was the cipher systems provided for use by corps signal intelligence companies were inadequate because of the time it took to encode and decode messages. They recommended cipher machines be used to speed the process of reporting intelligence to the commander.[221]

The Third Army SIS detachment made the following observations on radio intelligence activities:

a. Army and corps level RI units should work on messages of a higher grade. The SIS detachment felt the same as the 3254th. Often perishable intelligence information in a message of medium or high grade did not make its way to a subordinate commander in time. The two intelligence units noted above highlight that information processed and passed to either the corps or the army G-2. What is not seen is the information that may have been useful to a corps commander but was decoded too late to be of any use.[222]

The Third Army felt the corps' primary mission should concentrate on plain text and low grade cipher, with a secondary mission focused on medium grade traffic. The army level signal intelligence unit would then primarily concentrate on medium grade messages, with a secondary mission of breaking low grade traffic. Their opinion was that low grade traffic was of immediate value to a corps, of some utility to an army, but of no immediate importance to an army group. Likewise, medium grade traffic was of prime importance to an army commander.[223]

b. Another suggestion was to organize all signal intelligence organizations within an army into a battalion. The size of the companies would remain close to what they currently were, but it would allow the army level signal intelligence organization to manage resources across the board. It would allow the shifting of personnel and/or equipment as warranted by the tactical situation. It would also give the signal units the ability to cross level and ensure an equitable distribution of experienced personnel.[224]

c. One major criticism made by the Third Army SIS was that an officer in the G-2 section needed to be trained in signal intelligence matters. They found that the officer in charge of the army or corps radio intelligence unit had to personally pass on intelligence and assist in the evaluation process. This took the OIC away from his duties at his unit.[225]

This was one area that had been addressed before the war, yet nothing was done. Captain Garland C. Black, later to become a brigadier general and assigned as the signal officer for 12th Army Group in 1945, wrote of the need for a G-2 Signals Team in 1936 in the Signal Corps Bulletin. He recognized the unique nature of the information that could be provided by the signal company to the G-2. The previous war proved that the Signal Corps had a direct relation to military intelligence, and that it would be logical for the two staff officers, the G-2 and Signal Officer, to be joined together as a team. This would facilitate efficient staff cooperation and collaboration.[226]

CHAPTER FIVE - CONCLUSION AND ANALYSIS

Radio intelligence, or signals intelligence, evolved from World War I to the end of World War II as technology and its applications evolved. The arrival of the internal combustion engine and its revolution of modern warfare made radio a necessity. As combat forces became mechanized, their range, speed, and span of control grew proportionally. Radio became the mechanism to control these forces. German *blitzkrieg* tactics became the archetype of modern warfare.

As more nations used radio to control their forces, radio intelligence grew in importance. Nations learned from World War I the value of signal intercept. Here was a fountain of information that allowed a commander to peer into the mind of another commander. For the first time enemy intentions could be divined through the regular intercept, decoding, and reading of the opponent's messages.

In World War I radio intelligence remained at the theater army level. The First Army established an organization within the G-2 section to direct, coordinate, and interpret the results from the Signal Corps intercept activities. Publication of FM 11-20 in 1940 solidified the placement of radio intelligence units at a theater army, at a general headquarters, or at the war department staff. Radio intelligence made a significant contribution to the effort in World War II. The Army recognized the importance when they created additional radio intelligence companies to provide direct support to a corps commander. As the war progressed, the Army realized radio intelligence had a place within the tactical and operational spheres of command. Initially, armies and army groups had signal radio intelligence companies assigned. Later 12th Army Group created signal service companies from TO&E 11-500 in response to a support requirement at the corps level.

Analysis

The initial employment of radio intelligence at corps, army, and army group levels successfully exploited low level German cryptographic systems. American analysts could readily identify German units through call sign analysis and radio procedures (traffic analysis), and could obtain locations from the contents of the messages. This furnished essential order of battle information to intelligence officers.[227]

Radio intelligence, as developed in the European Theater of Operations (ETO), required a high degree of coordination between the corps, army, and army group intercept units. This coordination requirement was unforeseen by doctrine developers before the war. The initial concept of signal intelligence had one radio intelligence company supporting a theater army. The extensive use of radios in mechanized forces, particularly in the *Panzer* and mobile artillery units, gave commanders and intelligence officers a unique capability to track uncommitted enemy forces. Radio intelligence identified and forecasted the commitment of German reserves at threatened points before any other source of combat intelligence. A secondary benefit derived from the interception of German reconnaissance patrol communications. This information frequently detailed American positions, thus providing the corps and army commanders information of friendly movements before situation reports were received through normal distribution channels.[228]

While a key source of combat information, radio intelligence was not the Oracle of Delphi. There were, and are, several limitations of radio intelligence. Radio intelligence could be deceived through dummy traffic. While there are few known cases of German attempts to deceive American intelligence through dummy nets, the Allies proved this could be successful. As part of Operation "Fortitude" before the invasion of Europe, the Allies created a separate radio net in England. This gave the Germans the impression that another army group, with Patton as its commander, would invade France at Pas de Calais.[229]

Radio intelligence required a sustained effort. Results depended on a firm technical groundwork that had to be maintained even as the enemy changed procedures. Without knowledge of frequencies, call signs, codes, message protocols, and other technical details, intercept operators wandered aimlessly through the frequency spectrum searching for enemy transmissions. Only with proper technical data could their efforts be channeled against units posing the greatest threat to American formations.

Success came only from exploitation of enemy weaknesses in communications and cryptography. Some German units had weak radio security procedures. These were the easiest to exploit and gain intelligence. The 3rd *PanzerGrenadier* Division provided an excellent example of lax security and the information gained through radio intelligence. Others had an excellent signal security program, making American analysts work harder to develop combat information.

Similarly, General Praun believed that the German signal intelligence scored its greatest successes through Allied communication blunders. Radio discipline taught in the States deteriorated while American units were stationed in the United Kingdom. During the later stages of the war, discipline remained inconsistent throughout the army. The Germans believed Third Army units were by far the most lax, while the Fifteenth's had excellent radio security. Other units fell between those two extremes. The higher echelon nets were secure; most of the German successes came at the expense of insufficiently disciplined lower echelon nets.[230]

Until January 1945 the Germans selected their call signs and frequencies in a systematic method. This enabled analysts to maintain continuity on German units by predicting with some degree of accuracy the new frequencies and call signs. When a random selection method was introduced, the changes caused a considerable reorientation of effort. One operational change was the increased use of direction finders as part of traffic analysis and target continuity. The success of the Allies' February offensive, and the rapid disorganization of German forces in March and April 1945, lessened the effects of the German signal changes than if they had been made earlier in 1944.[231]

Another limitation of radio intelligence was its complete dependence on the cooperation of the enemy to transmit. Intelligence results were low when the volume of traffic intercepted diminished for any reason, such as atmospheric disturbance, local noise, a retreating front, or radio silence. The German counteroffensive through the Ardennes illustrated this limitation. Both ULTRA and army radio intelligence units did not provide indications of the attack. Most of the traffic intercepted by RI units was more of an administrative and routine nature; nothing suggested two *Panzer* armies were being readied for a strike.

The primary benefit of radio intelligence was the order of battle information provided to support the all-source intelligence effort. It allowed intelligence staffs to develop the situation within their areas of operations and influence. It supported the G-2's intelligence and warning mission by providing early warning of enemy movements. By analyzing and fusing SIGINT with other the sources of intelligence, the G-2 staff could acquire and nominate targets to the G-3, fire support officer and the commander. Employed on a common sense basis, radio intelligence gleaned every bit of intelligence from a unit's transmissions. This included the positions of his transmitters, the volume of traffic, net procedures, and message content.[232]

Two important developments occurred in the employment of radio intelligence in the ETO. The first development was the inclusion of an evaluation, or analysis, group as an organic part of radio intelligence companies. This group processed the traffic, deciphered what messages they could, and determined the order of battle. Their daily activity report went to their G-2. The addition of the evaluation group was a change in doctrine and practice as first employed in Italy and transferred later to France.[233]

The second development was the creation of the corps signal service companies to provide radio intelligence support. Their results, besides going directly to their G-2, went to the radio intelligence company at army level. This expanded the pool of intercept available to army and army group analysts. Technical coordination among all echelons of radio intelligence support resulted in a highly effective organization throughout the theater.[234]

During the Battle of the Bulge, signals intelligence played a key role in allowing senior Allied commanders to assess German intentions. Signal Security Detachment D concluded that messages from 13 German divisional formations in and near the Bulge were received. These formations represented the bulk of the armored and mechanized forces available to Hitler on the western front. The intelligence gained from their messages not only indicated their future activities, but also provided the G-2 with reliable information at a time when other intelligence sources were unproductive.[235]

Because of its perceived reliability, and because other sources of information were closed to them, the Germans paid more attention to radio intelligence training than did the Americans. The German intelligence officer and his commander wanted intelligence that provided an immediate tactical advantage. Radio intelligence provided this more than any other source. Both Generals Praun and Kesselring estimated that almost 95 percent of German intelligence came from signals intercept by the close of the war.[236]

Direction finding was not so important early in the Normandy invasion and subsequent campaign. Radio intelligence units had not received adequate training on deployment and employment of DF equipment. Early DF equipment weighed over 300 pounds. Systems developed as the war progressed weighed over one half ton. The army used trucks to transport the systems, but DF equipment in World War II never became truly portable.

When the Germans began changing their cryptographic systems in late 1944 to the *Rasterschluessel,* American analysts lost access to the information contained within the intercepted messages. This placed a greater burden on the traffic analysts and increased interest on information that could be obtained through direction finding. During the expansion of the Remagen bridgehead, the 113th RI company, supporting First US Army, tracked the movement and commitment of the *Panzer Lehr* and 341st Assault Gun Brigade through direction finding efforts. The army began to focus its attention on equipment, deployment, and employment difficulties of DF systems.[237]

Within the ETO army signal officers solved DF problems in a variety of methods. One solution mounted SCR-291 radio sets, an air traffic control radio, on trucks for DF purposes. The antenna sensitivity apparently was better than those of the current DF systems in use. However one major drawback to the SCR-291 was that it did not go below 1500 kilocycles; units still needed another system to cover the lower portion of the frequency spectrum. American RI units used British, or even captured German, vehicular mounted DF systems whenever they could. Units also became adept at developing field expedient methods to improve system capability. The Army Service Forces sent a team to Europe to modify DF sets based on homemade fixes developed by RI units in Italy.[238]

Captain Stuart Martin, Signal Corps, believed two DF

systems were sufficient for a corps radio intelligence unit. The small size of the signal service companies, generally around 120 men, did not support manning four or five outstations. The narrow corps frontage did not support operating an extended DF baseline. Knowing whether traffic originated from its immediate front satisfied the majority of the corps DF requirements. Traffic analysis would then help learn which enemy was in front of the corps.[239]

Direction finding could not provide locations to a degree accurate enough for directing artillery fire. Instead, with proper technique and analysis, it might have been possible to determine location to a four to five square kilometer circular error of probability. However, the army G-2 would know which units were astride his lines of operation, which units were the enemy's reserve, and how those units were moving.[240]

Conclusions

Though the U.S. Army understood the importance of radio intelligence, it was not the most important source of combat intelligence. The G-2 at the 12th Army Group listed SIGINT as the third most productive source of information after enemy prisoners of war *(EPW)* and aerial reconnaissance. Several factors explain why. Radio intelligence was a new source of combat information. Staff intelligence officers at all levels did not know how to incorporate it with the other sources. EPW interrogation was a more traditional source of intelligence. The G-2 had someone he could see and interrogate. He could then determine the validity of the information he received. The same goes for aerial reconnaissance. Though technologically new, it had the advantage of providing a physical product that the G-2 could touch and see. He could look at the photo and make his own decisions about the information it contained.

Radio intelligence provided no physical product in the traditional method of collection. Intelligence staff officers had to rely on the word of operators that what was written down was what the enemy transmitted. He could not physically touch, see, or smell the enemy's transmission. The newness of radio intercept put off many customers. Secretary of State Henry Stimson shut down his department's collection and decoding operations with his statement that gentlemen do not read each other's mail. Intelligence officers were also averse to radio intelligence. The 85th Division's G-2 stated that he considered radio intelligence entirely unnecessary. During the war, radio intelligence became an important part of all source intelligence. Either the G-2's staff learned to interpret the information or, more often than not, the SRI company sent a liaison officer to help interpret results and write future collection requirements.

During the western European campaigns radio intelligence did not need to be the primary source of combat information. Allied air supremacy allowed them to use aerial reconnaissance almost at will. The Allies were on the offensive and had greater opportunities to take German prisoners. Radio intelligence contributed to all source intelligence and increased the confidence factor in the overall product. It could alert intelligence officers to impending German actions, which could then be confirmed by aerial reconnaissance. Conversely other sources could also provide tip offs to radio collectors. This allowed analysts to figure out the enemy's intentions and capabilities, especially the *Panzer* and *PanzerGrenadier* units.

The Germans relied on SIGINT to a greater degree than the Americans. Their air reconnaissance was of limited value due to the overwhelming Allied air superiority. The Germans also had less of an opportunity to take prisoners as they were on the defensive awaiting Allied attacks. They emphasized tactical collection to increase their chances of survival. They developed the broadcast system to warn their frontline units of impending air, artillery, or ground attacks. Their use of radio intelligence increased their combat power by minimizing direct losses through Allied actions.

Today the Army needs to respond to technological advances just as it needed to fifty years ago. Radios are smaller because of microchips and solid state circuitry, and can be found throughout all levels of command. They communicate farther, faster, and more secure than their ancestors did. Enciphering devices are readily available as well. A small computer can generate algorithms for ciphers that can provide security during the critical period of any operation before they are broken. An investment in research and development is required to keep abreast of technological advances and to discover weaknesses to exploit.

The Army must take another look at how SIGINT support is provided to the various echelons. Gone are the days when simple codes, like the HST, can be broken and read at corps level or lower. Tactical requirements are now target acquisition and situation development. Direction finding and traffic analysis fulfill this requirement. It is doubtful if there is a future for cryptanalysts and linguists at the tactical echelons in the future. Instead the corps will have to place a greater reliance on theater and national assets providing the opposing commander's intentions.

Downsizing of the armed forces presents another challenge. Before World War II the Army's SIGINT capability consisted of seven stations intercepting diplomatic traffic. As the Army increased in size, it used TO&E 11-77 to build tactical radio intelligence companies to support field armies, but it was not enough. Using a celluar table of organization, TO&E 11-500, the Army created companies tailored specifically for certain missions. These companies were not only signal service companies, but they were construction companies, wire companies, and so forth.

A smaller army today may need the ability of celluar military intelligence organizations to create a force structure capable of meeting future challenges. Analysts, linguists, collection operators are among the many military occupational skills that can be organized into smaller cells with specific functions. For example, two analytic platoons could be created and maintained by a corps headquarters with two divisions assigned. In peacetime the two platoons provide direct support to the corps and its subordinate divisions. When a division deploys to a "hot spot," one analytic platoon goes with it and continues to provide dedicated support. This could reduce the number of platoons required by one.

Theater and national level intelligence assets must

assume the intelligence burden that once belonged within the purview of the corps and division G-2. A clear understanding of tactical and operational requirements is necessary to provide those commanders with the support they need. These organizations will not only fulfill strategic requirements, but they must push down intelligence to the appropriate level.

To protect the grand "left hook" maneuver during Desert Storm, tactical MI units at the corps level and below could not move close enough to the Iraqi border to collect information and develop their order of battle databases. Instead, these commanders and their staff relied on collection assets and analysts several levels removed to provide the answers to their priority intelligence requirements. Without leaving the continental United States, some national intelligence agencies provided support directly to the corps, divisions, and brigades in the field. Other agencies flew support teams into the theater to assist the command in interpreting information and stating requirements. Desert Storm provided a glimpse of the future of intelligence within the Army. The lesson learned from Desert Storm is the same as the lesson learned fifty years ago: Intelligence delayed or never received is intelligence wasted.

ENDNOTES

1. Department of the Army, <u>FM 100-5: Operations</u> (Washington, DC: US Government Printing Office), 1986, p. 130-31.

2. It is interesting to note that Hindenburg did not credit radio intelligence for his success at Tannenberg. Regardless of his feelings, there exists enough evidence to show that the Germans relied heavily on those intercepts, and others later in the war, to keep the Russians at bay. Flicke ensures readers are aware that Hindenburg did not devote one word to the intercepted radiograms in his book <u>Aus meinem Leben.</u> Flicke charges Hindenburg with describing "...the course of the Battle of Tannenberg in such fashion as to give the definitive impression that he was in the dark as to the enemy's objectives and organization." Wilhelm F. Flicke, <u>War Secrets in the Ether (volume I)</u> (Laguna Hills, CA: Aegean Park Press, 1977), 9. On the other hand, German commanders consistently avoided mentioning SIGINT in their memoirs. This could be viewed as simply good cover and deception, as well as protection of a lucrative intelligence source.

3. Oscar W. Koch, <u>G-2: Intelligence for Patton</u> (Philadelphia: Whitmore Publishing Co., 1971), 50-120. In these seventy

pages, covering the western European campaigns, the only mention remotely concerned with radio intelligence is on page 64. Here General Koch discusses being awaken by the G-2 duty officer that higher headquarters had information from "a usually reliable source" that a German counterattack was planned. This source could only be ULTRA.

4. Military Intelligence Division, U.S. War Department German Military Intelligence 1939-1945 (Frederick, MD: University Publications of America, 1984). Albert Praun, "German Radio Intelligence (Foreign Military Studies Manuscript P-038)," in German Radio Intelligence and the Soldatensender (Covert Warfare. No. 6), ed. John M. Mendelsohn (New York: Garland Publishing, Inc., 1989).

5. G. Dickson Gribble, Jr., "ULTRA: Its Operational Use in the European Theater of Operations, 1943-1945" (Carlisle Barracks, PA: US Army War College, 1991).

6. Samuel B. Griffith, trans. Sun Tzu: The Art of War (London: Oxford University Press, 1963), 84.

7. Fletcher Pratt, Secret and Urgent –The Story of Codes and Ciphers (New York: The Bobbs -Merrill Company, 1939), 236.

8. Ibid., 237.

9. Barbara W. Tuchman, The Guns of August (New York: MacMillan Publishing Co., Inc., 1962; Bantam Books, 1980),

324-27.

10. Having fortuitously obtained a copy of Lee's plans by capturing a courier who had wrapped the plans around his cigars, McClellan moved with surprising speed after learning of the plans to split the Confederate Army. The result was one of the bloodiest days in the Civil War, the battle of Sharpsburg, or Antietam Creek. Beringer, Richard E., et al, <u>Why the South Lost the Civil War</u> (Athens, GA: University of Georgia Press, 1986), 166-67.

11. Flicke, <u>War Secrets (vol. 1),</u> p. 12-13.

12. Ibid., 20.

13. Ibid., 23.

14. Ibid., 20-21.

15. Penelope S. Horgan, "Signals Intelligence Support to U.S. Military Commanders: Past and Present" (Carlisle Barracks, PA: U.S. Army War College, 1991), 14. See also John Patrick Finnegan, <u>Military Intelligence: A Picture History</u> (Arlington, VA: History Office, US Army Intelligence and Security Command, 1984), p. 13-14. Pancho Villa did not have any radios.

16. Army Security Agency, "Historical Background of the Signal Security Agency, Volume II: World War I." File SRH-001, Records of the National Security Agency, National

Archives Record Group #457 (hereafter referred to as SRH-001, Vol II), 173.

17. A. G. Reame, "Electronic Warfare in the Field Army: A Historical Analysis" (Ft Leavenworth, KS: US Army Command and General Staff College, 1964), 38-39.

18. Ibid., 39-40.

19. SRH-001, Vol II, 176.

20. Ibid., 177.

21. The Second Army Radio Intelligence Section was formed on 22 September 1918 by taking an officer and two clerks from the First Army's section. The taking of trained personnel from radio intelligence units to create another would repeat itself during World War II. They made all necessary preparations and submitted routine reports, but the signing of the armistice on 11 November 1918 left them unblooded. SRH-001, vol II, 196-97.

22. Reame, 40.

23. Ibid.

24. SRH-001, vol II, 179.

25. One. goniometric bearing (line of bearing) results in determining the general arrival direction of the signal. Two bearings on the same signal result in a "cut." While narrowing down the location of the transmitter, a cut is not accurate enough to take action. Three bearings from different

intercept/direction finding stations on the same signal result in a fix. A fix provides a definite location of the transmitter. More bearings on the same signal will decrease the circular error of probability and result in a more refined location of the transmitter. Goniometric stations are the same as direction finding in today's terms.

26. SRH-001, vol II, 185-6.

27. Ibid., 185.

28. American Expeditionary Forces, General Staff, Second Section, "Final Report of the Radio Intelligence Section, General Staff, General Headquarters, American Expeditionary Forces, 1918-1919" File SRH-014, Records of the National Security Agency, National Archives Record Group #457 (referred to as SRH-014), 26.

29. Ibid., 26.

30. Praun, 155.

31. SRH-014, 7.

32. The sites were located at Konigsberg (I), Stettin (II), Spandau (III), Dresden (IV), Stuttgart (V), Muenster (VI), Munich (VII), Frankfurt an der Oder (1), Breslau (2) Kassel (3), as well as at Nuernberg and Hanover. The Roman numerals designate military district headquarters; the Arabic numbers, cavalry division headquarters. Praun, 155.

33. *Traite De Paix Entre Les Puissances Alliees Et Associees Et L'Allemagne Et Protocole Signes A Versailles, Le 28 Juin 1919.* From the collection of Dr. S.J. Lewis, US Army Command and General Staff College, Fort Leavenworth, Kansas.

34. Praun, 156.

35. Ibid.

36. Ibid., 156-57.

37. Ibid., 157-58.

38. Ibid., 158-59.

39. Flicke, War Secrets (vol I), 92-93.

40. Praun, 159.

41. Ibid., 158-50. David Kahn, Hitler's Spies. German Military Intelligence in World War II. (New York: MacMillan Publishing Co., 1978), 198.

42. SRH-001, vol II, n.180.

43. Robert G. Angevine, "Gentlemen Do Read Each Other's Mail: American Intelligence in the Interwar Era," Intelligence and National Security 7, no. 2 (1992), 17.

44. William F. Friedman, "A Brief History of the Signal Intelligence Service, dated June 29, 1942." File SRH-029, Records of the National Security Agency, National Archives Record Group #457. (future references to SRH-029)

45. Angevine, 16-17.

46. Ibid., 17-18.

47. The six stations organized between 1930 and 1935 were Fort Monmouth, NJ (1st Radio Intelligence Company); Fort Sam Houston, TX (7th Signal Service Company); Presidio of San Francisco, CA (8th Signal Service Company); Fort Shafter, Territory of Hawaii (9th Signal Service Company); Fort McKinley, Philippines (10th Signal Service Company), and Quarry Heights, Canal Zone. By 1 January 1939, the companies were reassigned to the 2d Signal Service Company (later the 2d Signal Service Battalion) with its headquarters at Fort Monmouth, NJ. Angevine, 21. Also, Army Security Agency, The Origin and Development of the Army Security Agency 1917-1947 (Washington. DC. March 19481 (Laguna Hills, CA: Aegean Park Press, 1978), 23.

48. Angevine, 22.

49. Nigel West, The SIGINT Secrets: The Signals Intelligence War. 1900 to Today (New York: William Morrow and Company, Inc., 1988),-205-6.

50. George R. Thompson and Dixie R. Harris, The Signal Corps: The Outcome (Mid 1943 Through 19451 (Washington, DC: Office of the Chief of Military History, 1966), 348n.

51. The War Department was responsible for:

a. preparation of all means of secret communication employed by the Army in peace and war;

b. interception of enemy communications by electrical means, including necessary goniometric work; and,

c. the detection and solution of enemy secret communications, including codes, ciphers secret inks, and other methods employed.

The SIS at the General Headquarters level was responsible for the same functions as the War Department except that it prepared field codes and ciphers instead of army-level codes and ciphers. The field army SIS concentrated on interception and location of enemy signals and transmitters, and the solution of enemy codes and ciphers as assisted by SIS at General Headquarters. Army Security Agency, Origin 1917-1947, 10-11.

52. Ibid., 21.

53. W.D. Hamlin, Captain, "Organization and Training of the Third Radio Intelligence Company," The Signal Corps Bulletin, 108 (April-June 1940): 127-28.

54. United States. War Department, FM 11-20: Signal Corps Field Manual - Organization and Operations in the Corps, Army, Theater of Operations, and GHO (Washington, DC: War Department, 1940), 43.

55. Ibid., 43-5.

56. Ibid., 45-46.

57. Ibid., 47-9.

58. Ibid., 46-50.

59. Ibid., 80-81.

60. Ibid.

61. Ibid.

62. Ibid., 60.

63. United States. War Department, <u>FM 11-22: Sianal Operations in the Corps and Army</u> (Washington, DC: War Department, 1945), 45.

64. Ibid., 33-40. The signal section at army headquarters was the office of the army signal officer. Besides overseeing signal intelligence activities within the army, the signal section also had responsibility for signal training, supply, photography, and signal communications.

65. Ibid., 39-40.

66. United States, War Department, Memorandum from Office of the Chief Signal Officer dated June 2, 1943. Subject: Observer's Report, 1943 Maneuvers.

67. United States, War Department, Memorandum from Office of the Chief Signal Officer dated 22 June 1943. Subject: Observer's Report, 1943 Maneuvers.

68. George R. Thompson and Dixie R. Harris, The Signal Corps: The Outcome (Mid 1943 Through 1945) (Washington, D.C.: Office of the Chief of Military History, 1966), 25-26.

69. FM 11-22, 15.

70. Ibid., 15-16.

71. Army Security Agency, "Histories of Radio Intelligence Units, European Theater, September 1944 to March 1945," File SRH-228, Records of the National Security Agency, National Archives Control Number NN3-457-83-34 (hereafter referred to as SRH-228), 228-230.

72. Hamlin, 127-28.

73. Ibid., 128.

74. 116th Signal Radio Intelligence Company, History of the 116th Signal Radlo Intelligence Company from Date of Activation, 18 May. 1942 until V-J Day, 2 September, 1945, (Munich: R. Oldenburg, 1945), 78.

75. Ibid., 64.

76. Ibid., 62.

77. Ibid., 62-3.

78. Ibid., 64.

79. Ibid., .

80. SRH -228, 301-302.

81. US War Department, OCSigO Memo dated June 2, 1943.

Subject: Observer's Report, 1943 Maneuvers.

82. US War Department, OCSigO Memo dated 22 June 1943. Subject: Observer's Report, 1943 Maneuvers.

83. United States, Army Service Forces, Memorandum from Signal Corps Ground Signal Agency dated 16 October 1944, Subject: Report on organization, Operations, and Training of Signal Radio Intelligence Companies in ETOUSA.

84. Ibid.

85. Ibid.

86. Ibid.

87. Third United States Army, Signal Intelligence Service, "Third Army Radio Intelligence History in Campaign of Western Europe." SRH-042, Records of the National Security Agency, National Archives Record Group #457 (hereafter referred to as SRH -042).

88. SRH-228, 293-294.

89. Ibid., 122-124.

90. Ibid., 124-130.

91. Ibid., 228-29.

92. Ibid., 229-230.

93. United States, War Department Memorandum from Office of the Chief Signal Officer dated 12 August 1944, Subject: Signal Questionnaire Answered by Radio Intelligence

Companies (with 7 enclosures). Responses from the following units included in this file are the 124th, 114th, 128th, 116th, 113th, 121st Radio Intelligence Companies, and one other unidentified radio intelligence company. The 118th Radio Intelligence Company also responded and is covered within another file. The following questions were asked:

1. How are radio intercept stations utilized?

2. How are direction finding stations utilized?

3. How close to front is company able to operate?

4. Is there a requirement at the corps level for radio direction finding of enemy stations?

5. Is augmentation with traffic analysis personnel necessary? If so, how many?

6. Are present training doctrines suitable and adequate?

7. What shortages of T/O&E equipment exist in this organization?

8. What increase or decrease in T/0&E equipment is recommended?

9. Is the degree of training prior to arrival in theater adequate? If not, why not?

10. Are your radio sets operated remote controlled? Do you control all remote radio sets from one central location thus establishing a "Radio Control Central?"

11. Are your troops equipped with panels AP-50 or AP-50-A? Are these panels satisfactory?

12. What means are taken to identify troops to friendly airplane crews during daylight? During darkness? Any effort made to identify motor vehicles from the air, or is this desirable? If yes, should this identification be by removable panel or painted design?

13. Is it practical for Headquarters and Signal units to formulate an SOP and follow same in combat operations as a general rule?

14. What is the ability of signal equipment to perform functions intended for general service use to meet requirements peculiar to your particular theater?

15. How does the functioning of your unit in theater differ from that during maneuvers?

16. Is training of a specialist and unit training satisfactory upon arrival?

17. Do you have any general comments on organization, equipment, employment, maintenance and/or supply of signal communication not included in above questions?

94. Military Intelligence Division, German Military Intelligence 1939-1945, 151.

95. Ibid., 151.

96. Ibid., 5.

97. Ibid., 149.

98. Ibid., 155-59.

99. Ibid., 171.

100. United States War Department, Memorandum from Office of the Chief Signal Officer dated 24 October 1944. Subject: Intercept and its Application

101. Ibid.

102. Ibid.

103. Ibid.

104. United States Army Service Forces. Memorandum from Office of the Chief Signal Officer dated 24 October 1944, Subject: Employment of Radio Intelligence in Tactical Support of Army and Corps as Observed in Italy 11 May 1944 to 15 August 1944.

105. The Y Service was the British counterpart to the American radio intelligence. The Y Service intercepted and located enemy transmitters, conducted traffic analysis and low grade decryption much as we did. Many of our procedures came from observing and working with the British during the North African campaigns. SRH-228, 274. After intial radio intelligence failures by both the British and Americans during Operation TORCH, the British provided experienced SIGINT

personnel and units from other theaters to work with the American G-2 and radio intelligence organizations. The payoff came on 23 March 1943 when the 1st Infantry Division repulsed the 10th Panzer Division's counterattack in the El Guettar area. The Americans, commanded by LTG Patton, had been forewarned by intercept from the British Y unit with II US Corps. F. H. Hinsley, British Intelligence In the Second World War; Its Influnce on Strategy and Operations - Volume Two (New York: Cambridge University Press, 1981), 601, 743 46.

106. 12th Army Group, "History, Signal Section, 12th Army Group (FUSAG)," Historical Documents World War II (AGO Microfilm; Job No. 500), reel No. 115, item 1339.

107. United States, War Department. Table of Organization no. 11-77, Signal Radio Intelligence Company (Washington, DC: US Government Printing Office, 1942), 4.

108. The 3254th Signal Service Company organized their intercept platoon into three tricks. SRH-228, 230.

109. SRH-042, 5-7.

110. SRH-228, 92.

111. SRH-042, 12-13.

112. Ibid, 7.

113. Ibid., 8.

114. SRH-228, 207.

115. Ibid., 188.

116. SRH-042, 8.

117. SRH-228, 95-96.

118. Ibid., 231.

119. United States Army Service Forces. Officer of the Chief Signal Officer, "Direction Finders," Signal Corps Technical Information Letter 37 (December 1944), 7.

120. SRH-228, 231.

121. Ibid., 92.

122. Ibid., 93-94.

123. SRH-042, 009.

125. Ibid., 11-12.

126. Ibid., 11-12.

127. Ibid., 14-15.

128. SRH-228, 101-102.

129. Ibid.

130. SRH-042, 21-22. Also SRH-228, 186 and 267.

131. Gary B. Griffin, The Directed Telescope: A Traditionpl Element of Effective Command (1985; Reprint Ft Leavenworth, KS: U.S. Army Command and General Staff College, 1991), 25.

132. SRH-042, 24.

133. SRH-228, 88.

134. Ibid., 166-176.

135. Ibid., 136-138.

136. Ibid., 138.

137. Ibid., 140.

138. Ibid.,141.

139. Ibid., 141-142.

140. Ibid., 142-143.

141. Ibid., 143-144.

142. Ibid., 145-147.

143. V Corps Historical Section, "V Corps in the ETO 6 January 1942 - 9 May 1945," 136.

144. SRH-228, 299.

145. Ibid., 291.

146. Ibid., 308.

147. 12th Army Group, Report of Operations (Final After Action Report), vol IX Headquarters Commandant Section and Special Troops, 78.

148. SRH-228, 344-55.

149. Ibid., 264.

150. Ibid., 266-67.

151. Ibid., 270-71.

152. Ibid., 274.

153. Ibid., 60-61.

154. Ibid., 62.

155. Ibid., 64.

156. Ibid., 36-37.

157. Ibid., 9-11.

158. Ibid., 37.

159. Ibid., 39-40.

160. Ibid., 42-43. Kampfgruppen were temporary tactical organizations designed for a specific mission. They were similar to the combat commands or regimental combat teams used by American Divisions.

161. Ibid., 43-44.

162. Ibid., 45-46.

163. Ibid., 47.

164Ibid., 49-50.

165. Ibid., 50.

166. Ibid., 52.

167. Ibid., 53.

168. Ibid., 55.

169. Ibid., 56.

170. Ibid., 232.

171. Ibid., 234-34.

172. Ibid., 238-39.

173. Ibid., 242-43.

174. Ibid., 245-46.

175. Ibid., 247.

176. Ibid., 248.

177. Ibid., 250-51.

178. David Kahn, "German Military Eavesdroppers" <u>Cryptologia</u> (October 1977), 378. Bitzer stated that intercepted messages were sent to the KAST *(Korps Auswerte Staffel - corps evaluation staff)* of the LXXXII Corps. Messages that could not be deciphered at their level were passed to the AAST *(Armee Auswerte Staffel - army evaluation staff)* which had better facilities for decoding and evaluating mesages.

179. Military Intelligence Division, <u>German Military Intelligence 1939-1945,</u> 149-50.

180. Ibid., 287.

181. Praun, 83.

182. Ibid., 166-67.

183. Ibid., 164-65.

184. Ibid., 164.

185. Ibid.

186. Ibid., 165-66.

187. Ibid., 166.

188. Ibid., 73.

189. Ibid., 73-74.

190. Ibid., 75.

191. Ibid., 76-77.

192. Kahn, Hitler's Spies, 207.

193. Praun, 76-77.

194. Kahn, Hitler's Spies, 207.

195. Ibid., 207-8.

196. Kahn, Cryptologia, 379.

197. Praun, 81.

198. Ibid., 82.

199. Ibid., 84.

200. Ibid., 85. Also Kahn, Hitler's Spies, 208.

201. Kahn, Cryptologia, 379.

202. United States War Department, Memorandum from Office of the Chief Signal Officer dated 19 April 1945. Subject: PW Intelligence Bulletin No. 2/38 - Signal Intelligence.

203. Ibid.

204. Ibid.

205. Ibid.

206. Ibid.

207. Ibid.

208. SRH-228, 032.

209. Ibid. Also see United States Army Service Forces, Signal Corps Engineering Laboratories Memorandum dated 6 August

1945, Subject: Report on Direction Finding Operations in the European Theatre of Operations.

210. Ibid.

211. SRH-228, 032A.

212. Ibid.

213. Ibid., 032A-032B.

214. Ibid., 032B-033.

215. Ibid., 033.

216. Ibid., 34.

217. Ibid., 034-035.

218. Ibid.,036.

219. Ibid., 257.

220. Ibid., 257-58.

221. Ibid., 258.

222. Ibid., 60.

223. Ibid., 60-61.

224. Ibid., 60.

225. Ibid., 063.

226. Garland C. Black, Captain, "The G-2 Signals Team." The Signal Corps Bulletin 90 (May-June 1936), 24-5.

227. United States Army Service Forces, Signal Corps Engineering Laboratories Memorandum dated 6 August 1945, Subject: Report on Direction Finding Operations in the

European Theatre of Operations.

228. Ibid.

229. Ibid. John Keegan, The Second World War (New York: Penguin Books, USA Inc., 1990), 373.

230. Praun, 140-45.

231. Ibid.

232. United States Army Service Forces, Memorandum from Office of the Chief Signal Officer, Plans and Operations Division; Subject: Report of Trip to Italy - 24 October 1944.

233. USASF Signal Corps Memorandum, 6 August 1945, Subj: Report on DF Operations in the ETO.

234. Ibid.

235. Army Security Agency, "Examples of Intelligence Obtained from Cryptanalsis, 1 August 1946" (File SRH-066, Records of the National Security Agency, National Archives Control Number NN3-457-81-3. Reprinted in US Army Command and General Staff College, A627 Book of Readings, 125-137. Ft Leavenworth, KS: US Army Command and General Staff College, 1982.), 135. Keep in mind that aerial reconnaissance was ineffective due to weather in the first few days of the battle.

236. Praun, 95.

237. USASF Signal Corps Memorandum, 6 August 1945, Subj:

Report on DF Operations in the ETO.

238. Captain Stuart Martin and Mr. Pete O'Brien travelled to the ETO and visited the RI units supporting 12th Army Group; 1st, 3rd, 6th, 7th, and 9th Armies; and III, V, VI, and VII Corps. Their mission was to remedy equipment difficulties at corps level, and then improve equipment and operations at the army level. USASF Signal Corps Memorandum, 6 August 1945, Subj: Report on DF Operations in the ETO.

239. Ibid.

240. USASF Memo Subj: Report of Trip to Italy - 24 October 1944.

APPENDIX A

3250TH SIGNAL SERVICE COMPANY RESULTS OF INTERCEPT

The following charts provide an indication of the amount of intercept collected by a corps signal service company. The data is taken from the 3250th's company journal where a clerk wrote down the day's totals. There was no indication of the type of traffic, enemy units copied, or importance of the intercept as it related to V Corps maneuvers.

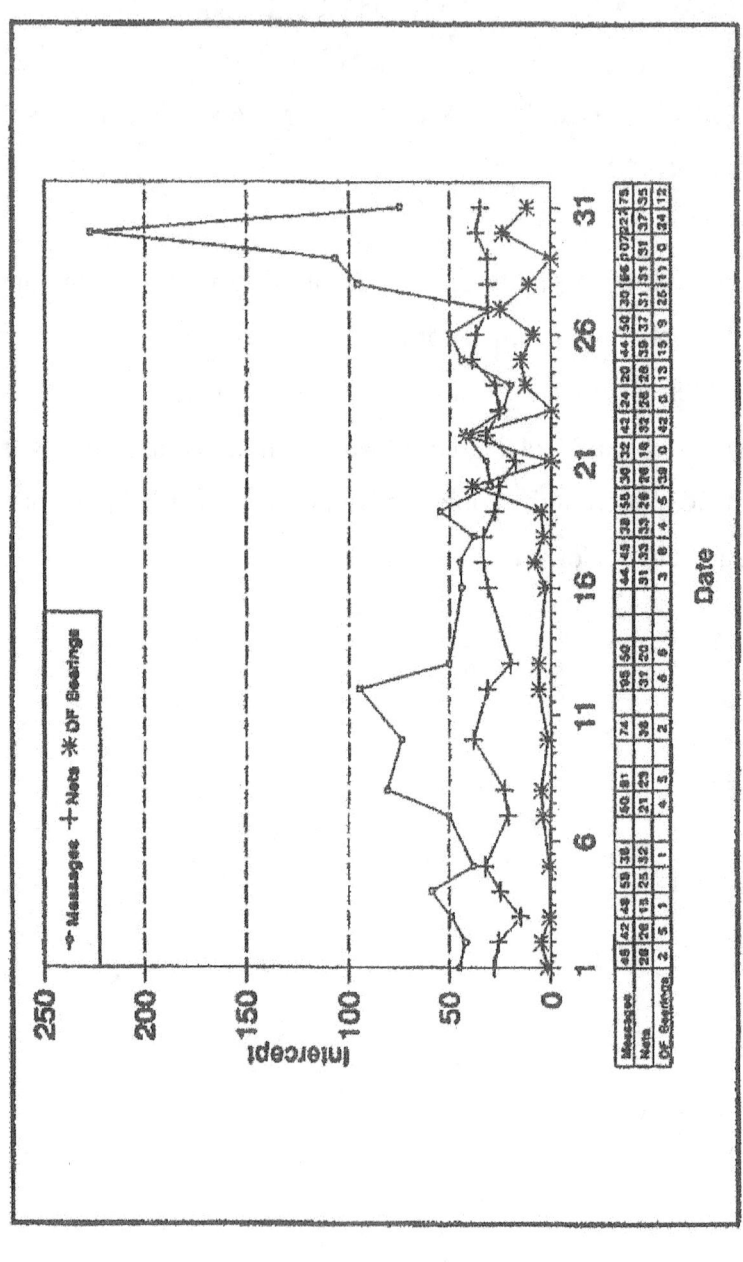

3250th Signal Service Company intercept results for July 1944 (Source: SRH-228).

The low level of DF bearings at the beginning of the month can be attributed to the problems the 3250th had with getting wire to the DF outstations, and the use of landline communiations by the Germans. The number of DF bearings increases at the end of the month as Operation COBRA kicks in and the Allies begin the breakout. The Germans were dislodged from their fixed positions and were forced to use the radio to control their forces.

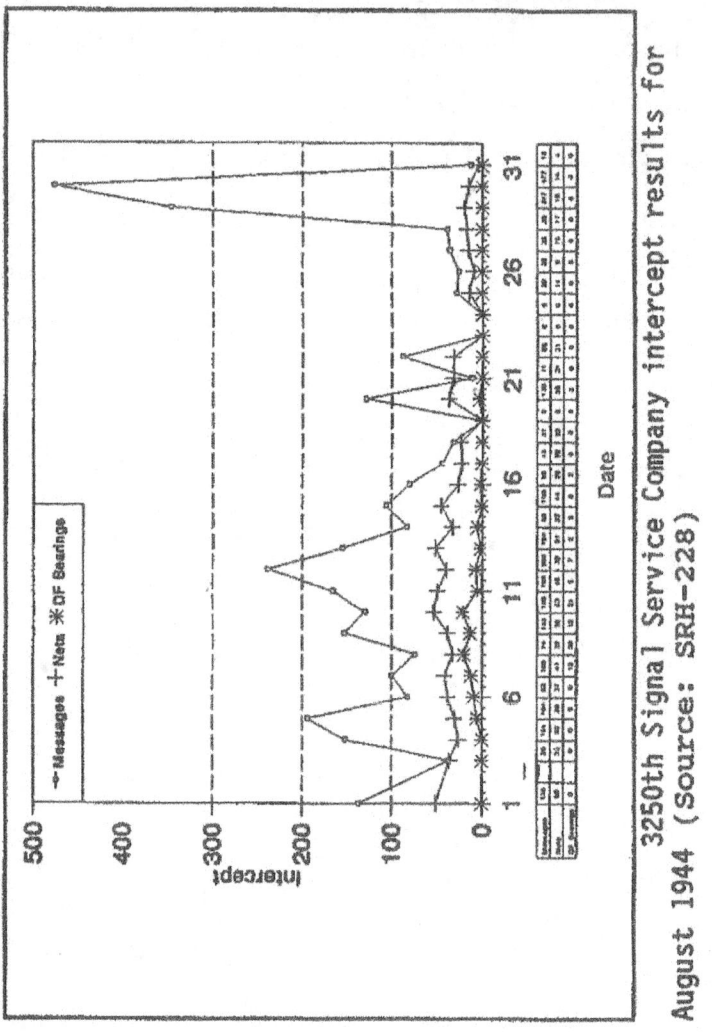

3250th Signal Service Company intercept results for August 1944 (Source: SRH-228)

The August message counts remain relatively high as the Germans were forced back from the Normandy area. The

Allied pursuit was in high gear. DF bearings were low because of the rapid forward movement of the corps. The DF outstations would reach their position, only to find they were out of range of the enemy signals again.

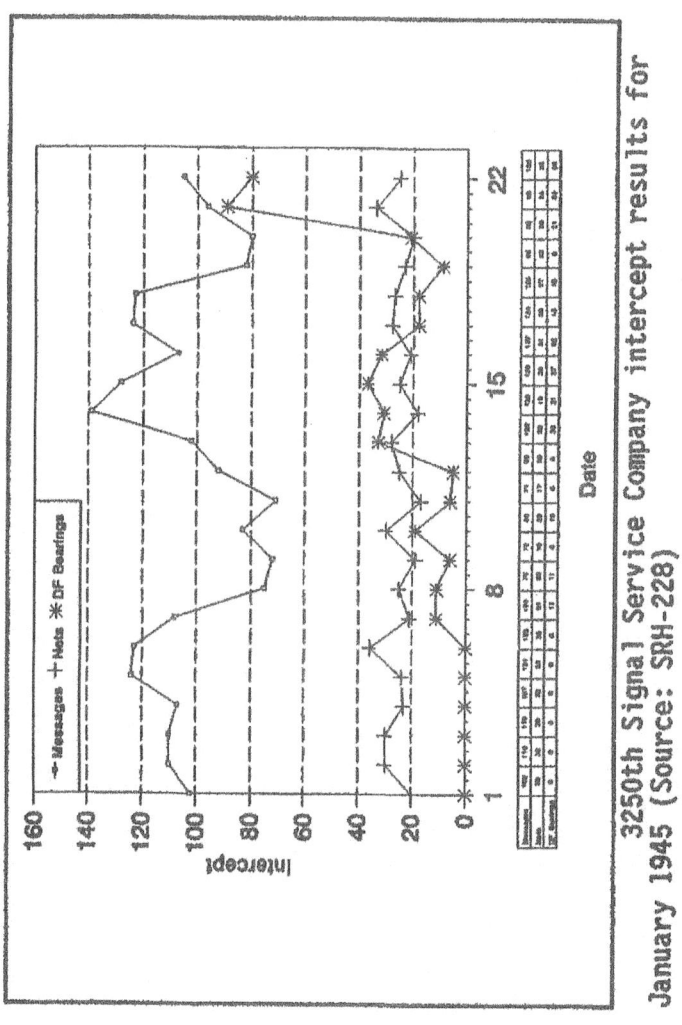

3250th Signal Service Company intercept results for January 1945 (Source: SRH-228)

The results for January remained consistently high for the first three weeks. The Allies had begun their counterattacks to reduce the Bulge salient. Because the Germans were on the offensive, they had to rely again on radio to control their forces. In their positions behind the West Wall they used landline again as the main means of communication. The number of nets intercepted remained fairly constant throughout the month. This can be attributed to the narrow focus of the company to collect against those units within the salient.

APPENDIX B

TABLES OF ORGANIZATION - SIGNAL RADIO INTELLIGENCE COMPANIES

The following pages provide a quick overview of how the organization of a radio intelligence company evolved between 1918 and 1942.

TABLE OF ORGANIZATION
ARMY RADIO SECTION, SIGNAL CORPS
T/O 232 -- 1918

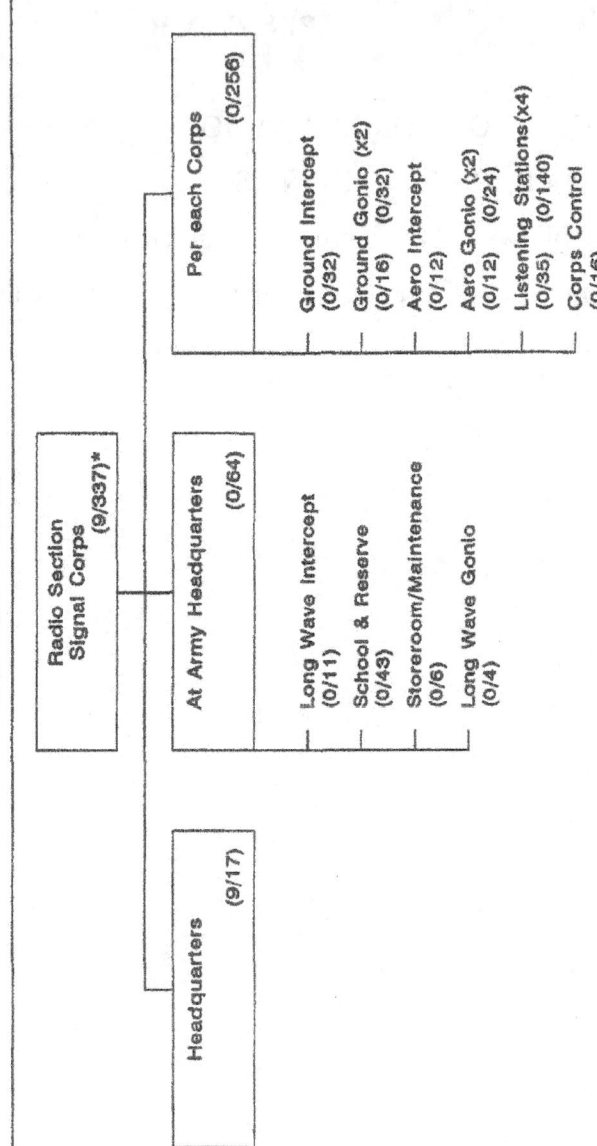

Radio Section
Signal Corps
(9/337)*

Headquarters
(9/17)

At Army Headquarters
(0/64)

Long Wave Intercept
(0/11)

School & Reserve
(0/43)

Storeroom/Maintenance
(0/6)

Long Wave Gonio
(0/4)

Per each Corps
(0/256)

Ground Intercept
(0/32)

Ground Gonio (x2)
(0/16)   (0/32)

Aero Intercept
(0/12)

Aero Gonio (x2)
(0/12)   (0/24)

Listening Stations(x4)
(0/35)   (0/140)

Corps Control
(0/16)

* (Officers/Enlisted men)

146

TABLE OF ORGANIZATION
RADIO COMPANY, SIGNAL CORPS
T/O 211W -- 1925

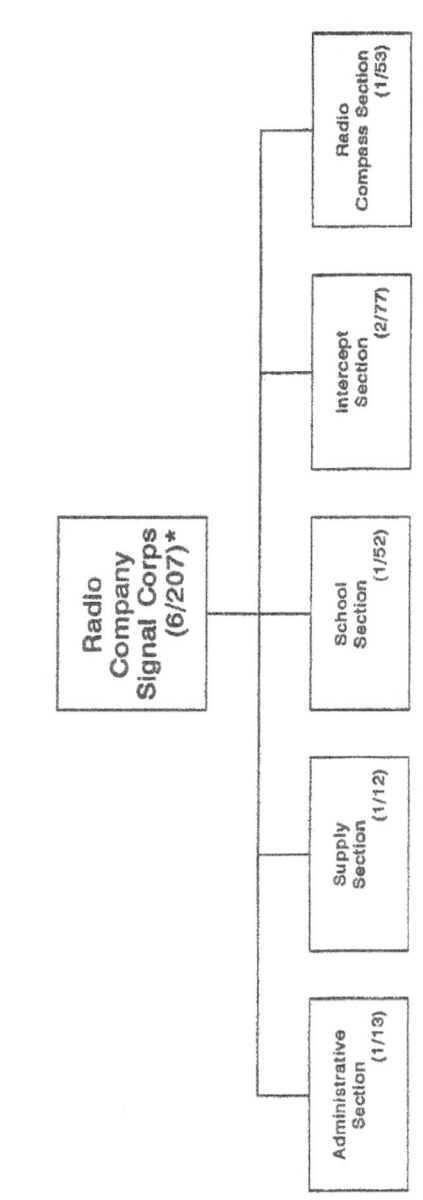

* (Officers/Enlisted men)

147

TABLE OF ORGANIZATION
RADIO COMPANY, SIGNAL CORPS
T/O 211W – 1930

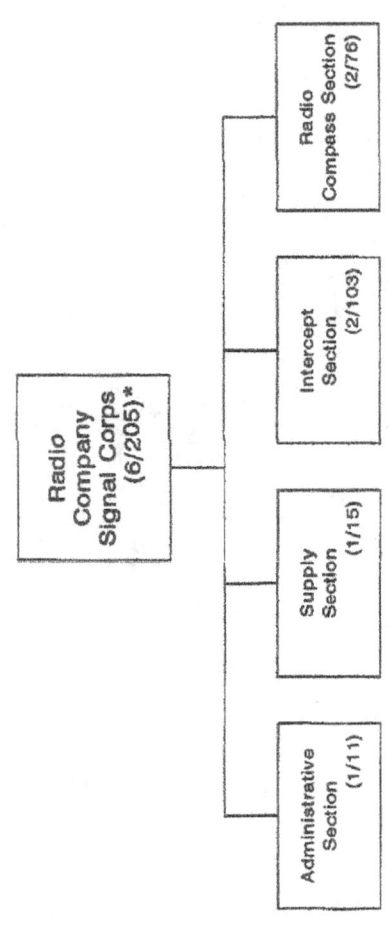

* (Officers/Enlisted men)
Superceded Table 211W dated 1925

TABLE OF ORGANIZATION
SIGNAL COMPANY, RADIO INTELLIGENCE
T/O 11-77 -- 1939

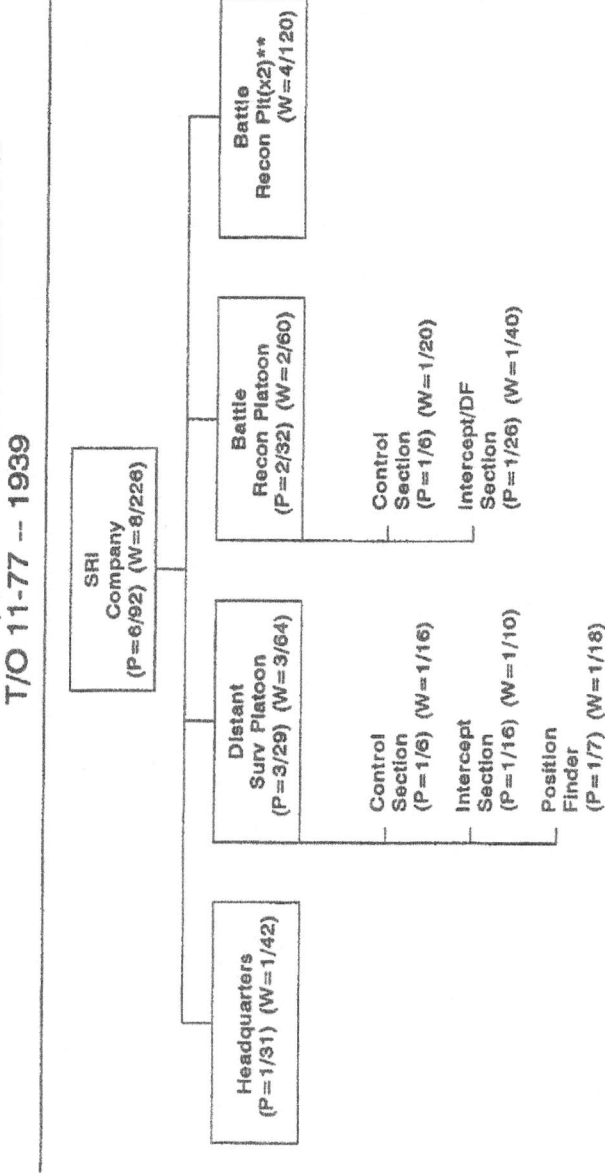

* (Officers/Enlisted men)

Superceded Table 211W dated 1930

** Two additional Battle Recon plts added for wartime organization.

TABLE OF ORGANIZATION
SIGNAL COMPANY, RADIO INTELLIGENCE
T/O 11-77 -- 1942

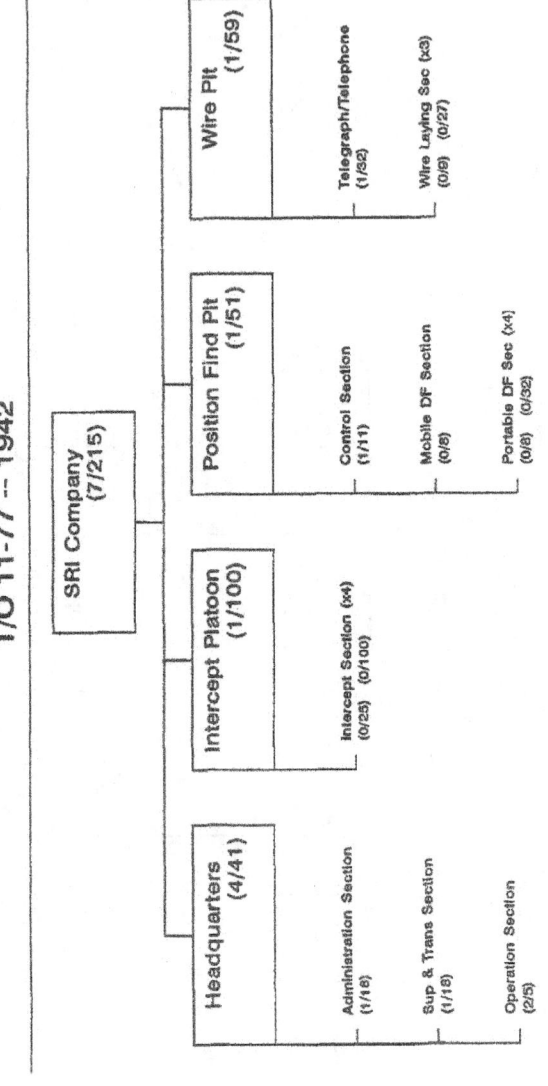

* (Officers/Enlisted men)
Superceded T/O 11-77 dated 1940

APPENDIX C

DIRECTION FINDING EQUIPMENT

The following information came from Signal Corps Technical Information Letter no. 37, December 1944.

{United States Army Service Forces, Officer of the Chief Signal Officer, "Direction Finders." Signal Corps Technical Information Letter 37 (December 1944): 7-10.}

Loop Antenna DF Systems

There were two types of DF antennas used in Army, the Loop and Adcock. The loop equipment was used for short range, weighed less, and was used in small bulk application. For a loop to operate satisfactory, it needed to be within a distance of transmitter where it can receive majority of the ground wave. The three loop DF antenna systems in use were:

a. **SCR-206-()**: a simple loop employing aural null indicating the bearing.

1. Frequency range: 0.2mc to 18.0mc. (One megacycle (mc) equals 1000 kilocycles (kc).)

2. Weight: approx 300 pounds of all equipment (includes power

source).

3. Consisted of a 15 inch loop with an azimuth scale mounted on top of receiver.

b. **SCR-503-()**: a crossed loop employing crossed pointer meter indication of bearing.

1. Frequency Range: 0.lmc to 3.0mc

2. Weight: 300 pounds for each; 600 pounds total for system.

3. Conisted of two separate units, each one a complete DF system. One unit covered the range of 0.lmc to 1.0mc, other covered the range of 1.0 to 3.0mc. Each unit had two 8 inch loops crossed at 90 degree angle, with an azimuth scale mounted on twin channel receiver. Outputs of each channel fed to one movement of a dual movement meter. The loops were rotated until the two movements aligned on a center line, thus indicating the bearing.

c. **SCR -504 -()**: Hand portable DF/homing set

1. Frequency range:

2. Weight: of DF equip - 26 pounds; weight of entire package - 80 pounds.

3. Consisted of radio receiver and small single loop antenna housed in a suitcase. It was designed to mask the true nature of equipment. It did not have an azimuth indicator since it was used more as a homing device. The operator then rotated the set

by hand until "null" is heard.

Adcock Antenna DF Systems

The Adcock direction finding units employed an antenna system that was not susceptible to large polarization errors. It could obtain signals where loop would not work (i.e., further towards rear). The Adcock antenna was extremely bulky. The following are Adcock antenna DF systems:

d. **SCR-255-()**: a rotatable H-Adcock DF

1. Frequency range: .34mc to 30mc.

2. Weight: 1200 pounds when set up for operation.

3. Antenna consisted of a notable H Adcock system with a 24 foot dipole spacing feeding into a National NC-100 receiver. The antenna, receiver, and two 6 volt storage batteries, and a loudspeaker, were mounted on top of a 15 foot wooden tower. The operator rotated the antenna through remote mechanical controls.

e. **SCR-551-()**: a rotatable elevated H-Adcock DF. It provided left and right cathode ray indication of bearing.

1. Frequency range: 2.0 to 20.0mc

2. Weight: 1200 pounds when set up for operation.

3. Consisted of an elevated H-Adcock antenna with receiver, indicator, and operator's position mounted on top of 15 foot

wooden tower. The operator's position was enclosed in a circular plywood shelter. The system operated on a switched cardiod principle. The indication of bearing, or azimuth, was obtained when two vertical traces on a cathode ray tube were of equal amplitude (height).

f. **SCR-555-()** and **SCR-556-()**: "twin systems"

1. Frequency range: 555: 18.0-65.0mc; 556: 65.0- 156.0mc.

2. Weight: unspecified in the article.

3. Both systems were a rotatable H-Adcock on a 14 foot wooden tower. The antenna was connected to a receiver and an indicator located at base of tower in a plywood shelter. The operator's position was located on the ground within the shelter. The equipment operated on a switched cardiod principle, with the indication of bearing obtained when the needle of a zero center type meter is in the zero position.

g. **SCR-291-()**: crossed U-Adcock antennas that provided instantenous bearing. It was used primarily for aircraft navigation, though some sets were issued to RI units.

1. Frequency range: 1.5 - 10.0mc, that could be extended to 20mc if properly employed.

2. Weight: 4000 pounds

3. The input from the antenna fed into a radiogoniometer. The output of the goniometer went to a receiver where it was

amplified and detected. The receiver output fed into deflecting ray coils of a cathode ray tube (spinning at same speed as goniometer). This caused a "Propeller trace" on a Cathode ray tube screen. The edge of the tube was graduated from 0 to 360 degrees. The operator read the strongest spike in the propeller to determine the bearing.

h. **SCR-502-()**: crossed U-Adcock; it also provided instantaneous bearing on a cathode ray tube.

1. Frequency range: 1.5 to 30.0mc

2. Weight:5000 pounds.

3. Very similar to SCR-291, but it had a larger antenna array to cover increased frequency range.

Accessories

The Loop Assembly AS-4()/GR was an attachment that, when attached to a receiver in freq range of 1.2 to 20.0mc., provided left-right indication of bearing on a double "magic eye" tube. The AS-4 has four 9 inch loops, an omnidirectional antenna, and a control box with azimuth scale. The loop covering the desired frequency range was mounted on the control box, which was connected to the receiver. The equipment was then ready to function. It weighed 80 pounds with its carrying case and four loops.

The use of the Loop Antenna Kit AS-169()/GR with the AS-4 assembly increased the frequency range to 0.075 - 20.0mc. The AS-169 had 4 additional loops to cover the 0.073 to 1.2mc range, and weighed just over 20 pounds with its carrying case and four loops.

APPENDIX D
UNIT CITATION AND CAMPAIGN PARTICIPATION

(Source: Department of the Army Pamphlet 672-1. Unit Citation and Campaign Participation Register. Washington, DC; July 1961.)

113th Signal Radio Intelligence Battalion [First Army]
Campaigns: Ardennes-Alsace

113th Signal Radio Intelligence Company [First Army]
Campaigns: Central Europe, Normandy, Northern France, Rhineland
Meritorious Unit Citation: 6 June - 6 August 1944, General Orders No. 22, HQs 1st US Army, dated 8 February 1945.
Occupation: 2 May - 30 September 1945 Germany

114th Signal Radio Intelligence Company [12th Army Group]
Campaigns: Ardennes-Alsace, Central Europe, Northern France, Rhineland
Occupation: 2 May - 27 December 1945 Germany

116th Signal Radio Intelligence Company [12th Army

Group]

Campaigns: Ardennes-Alsace, Central Europe, Northern France, Rhineland

Occupation: 2 May - 27 December 1945 Germany

117th Signal Radio Intelligence Company [Seventh Army]

Campaigns: Ardennes-Alsace, Central Europe, Rhineland, Rome-Arno, Southern France, Tunisia

Meritorious Unit Citation: 1 January - 31 March 1945, General Orders No. 389, HQs 7th US Army, dated 10 August 1945.

Assault Landing: Southern France, 15-16 August 1944, War Department General Orders No. 70-45.

118th Signal Radio Intelligence Company [Third Army]

Campaigns: Ardennes-Alsace, Central Europe, Normandy, Northern France, Rhineland

Meritorious Unit Citation: 1 August - 19 November 1944, General Orders No. 102, HQs 3rd US Army, dated 3 December 1944.

Occupation: 2 May - 27 December 1945 Germany.

121st Signal Radio Intelligence Company [ETOUSA COMMZ?]

Campaigns: Central Europe, Rhineland

Meritorious Unit Citation: 1 June - 31 July 1944, General Orders No. 28, HQs Communication Zone, European Theater of Operations, dated 11 March 1945.

Occupation: 2 May - 15 August 1945 Germany

124th Signal Radar (Radio?) Intelligence Company [ETOUSA, COMMZ?]

Campaigns: Central Europe, Rhineland

Meritorious Unit Citation: 1 January - 31 July 1944, General Orders No. 28, HQs Communication Zone, European Theater of Operations, dated 11 March 1945.

Occupation: 2 May - 15 August 1945 Germany.

129th Signal Radio Intelligence Company [6th Army Group]

Campaigns: Ardennes-Alsace, Central Europe, Rhineland

Occupation: 2 May - 31 October 1945 Germany

135th Signal Radio Intelligence Company [12th Army Group]

Campaigns: Central Europe, Rhineland

Occupation: 5 July - 31 October 1945 Germany

{The 135th SRI was under the 12th Army group for training

159

before assignment to the Fifteenth Army. The war ended before the 135th transferred to their new headquarters.}

137th Signal Radio Intelligence Company [Ninth Army]

Campaigns: Ardennes-Alsace, Central Europe, Northern France, Rhineland

Meritorious Unit Citation: 1 April - 18 August 1944, General Orders No. 34, HQs, Communication Zone, European Theater of Operations, dated 17 March 1945.

3250th Signal Service Company [V Corps]

Campaigns: Ardennes-Alsace, Central Europe, Normandy, Northern France, Rhineland

Assault Landing: Normandy, 6-7 June 1944, War Department General Orders 70-45.

3251st Signal Service Company [VII Corps]

Campaigns: Ardennes-Alsace, Central Europe, Normandy, Northern France, Rhineland

Meritorious Unit Citation: 6 June - 6 August 1944, General Orders No. 3, HQs VII Corps, dated 20 January 1945.

Occupation: 2 May - 5 July 1945 Germany

3252nd Signal Service Company [XIX Corps]

Campaigns: Ardennes-Alsace, Central Europe, Normandy, Northern France, Rhineland

Occupation: 2 May - 30 October 1945 Germany

3253rd Signal Service Company [XV Corps]

Campaigns: Ardennes-Alsace, Central Europe, Normandy, Northern France, Rhineland, Rome-Arno

Occupation: 2 May - 3 September 1945 Germany

3254th Signal Service Company [VIII Corps]

Campaigns: Ardennes-Alsace, Central Europe, -Normandy, Northern France, Rhineland

Occupation: 2 May - 3 September 1945 Germany

3255th Signal Service Company [XII Corps]

Campaigns: Ardennes-Alsace, Central Europe, Northern France, Rhineland, North Apennines, Po Valley

Occupation: 2 May - 31 October 1945 Germany

3256th Signal Service Company [XX Corps]

Campaigns: Ardennes-Alsace, Central Europe, Northern France (as the Signal Service Radio Intelligence Company), Rhineland

Occupation: 2 May - 14 August 1945 Germany

3257th Signal Service Company [XVI Corps]

Campaigns: Central Europe, Rhineland

Occupation: 2 May - 31 October 1945 Germany

3258th Signal Service Company [XIII Corps]

Campaigns: Ardennes-Alsace, Central Europe, Rhineland

Occupation: 2 May - 31 October 1945 Germany

3259th Signal Service Company [III Corps]

Campaigns: Central Europe, Rhineland

Occupation: 20 May - 14 August 1945 Germany

3260th Signal Service Company [VI Corps]

Campaigns: Ardennes-Alsace, Central Europe, Rhineland

3261st Signal. Service Company [XXI Corps]

Campaigns: Central Europe, Rhineland

Occupation: 2 May - 14 August 1945 Germany

3262nd Signal Service Company [XXII Corps]

Campaigns: Central Europe, Rhineland

Occupation: 2 May - 5 July 1945 Germany

3263rd Signal Service Company [XXIII Corps]

Campaigns: Central Europe

Occupation: 2 May - 30 October 1945 Germany

Signal Security Detachment D [12th Army Group]

Occupation: 2 May - 30 September 3.945 Germany

3201st Signal Intelligence Service Detachment [6th Army Group]

Campaigns: Ardennes-Alsace, Central Europe, Rhineland, Southern France

Occupation: 2 May - 31 October 1945 Germany

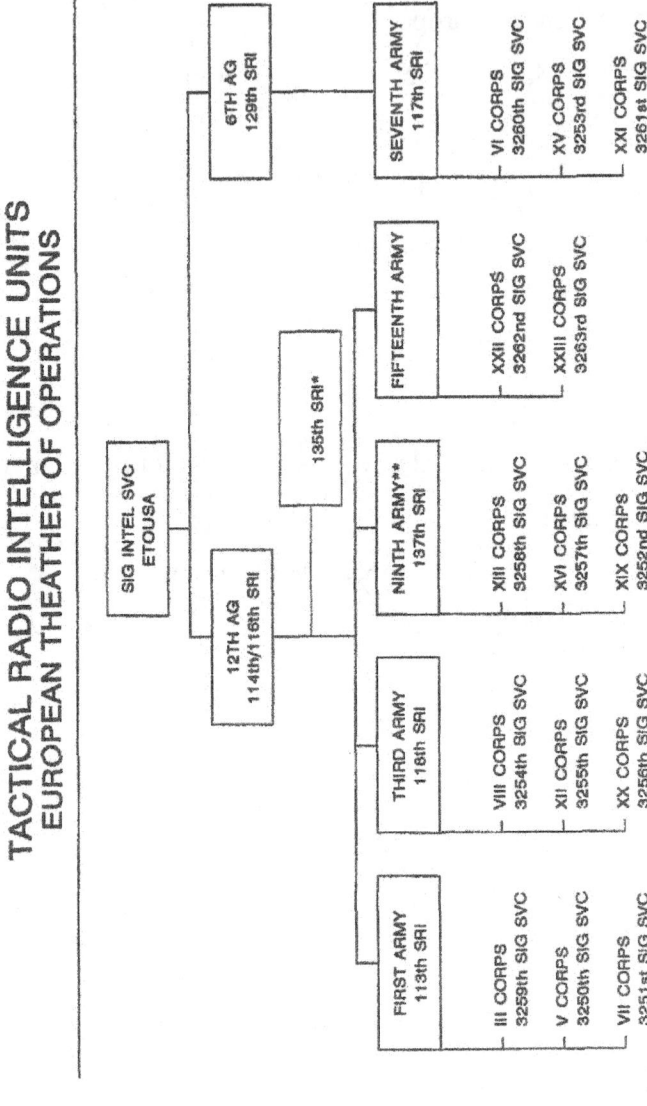

TACTICAL RADIO INTELLIGENCE UNITS
EUROPEAN THEATHER OF OPERATIONS

*135th ASSIGNED UNDER 12th AG FOR TRAINING BEFORE ASSIGNMENT TO FIFTEENTH ARMY.
**NINTH ARMY SOMETIMES UNDER 21st AG; 137TH RECEIVED TECHNICAL DIRECTION FROM 1 (BR) SIGNAL INT CO.

APPENDIX E

SEQUENCE OF COLLECTION OPERATIONS

A typical sequence as identified in FM 11-20 (1940 version) of operations would be as follows:

a. Initially the intercept operators are furnished copies of friendly call signs and frequencies in the bands they are to search. This allows quick identification of a signal as either friendly or enemy.

b. As an example, an operator is assigned to search the 3000-4000 kilocycle (kc) band, and hears an enemy station on a frequency of 3600 kc. He then notifies the control chief and begins to copy the message.

c. The control chief then verifies that the station at 3600 kc is an enemy transmitter. He must decide whether to continue with the copy or to drop coverage. (For the purpose of this sequence, the station is to be copied and located through direction finding.)

d. The control chief provides the four direction finding stations the frequency, call sign, mode of transmission, and any other data needed to recognize the signal and obtain an azimuth.

e. The four DF operators tune their receivers to the proper frequency, identify the signal, and determine the line of bearing from their location to the transmitter. If possible, the intercept operator puts the signal on the telephone wire to make it easier for the DF operators to identify the transmission. Once they obtain the line of bearing, the DF stations report the azimuth back to the control section.

f. The plotter at the control section corrects the azimuths with each station's calibration chart, plots the revised azimuths, and determines the coordinates of the transmitter. (Calibration charts were required regardless of where the DF site was located. These charts contained the corrections in degrees which should be added or subtracted from the observed azimuth to obtain the true azimuth. A minimum of two charts would be prepared, one below 4000 kc and one above. After accurately oriented the DF station and locating it on a map, a target transmitter is sent towards the front of the sector that is to be covered. The target transmitter transmits at given frequencies for about five minutes from sites easily located on the map. The differences from the map azimuths (from the DF site to the transmitter location) and the observed azimuths (the line of bearing obtained through DF) are plotted on a chart. For greater accuracy, and if time permits, the target transmitter transmits on several frequencies at each location, and then repeats the process at different times.)

g. The platoon leader sends the information, either by calling or by message, to the company headquarters. One copy of the message is then forwarded up channels. The second copy is retained for the consolidated log.

APPENDIX F

RADIO INTELLIGENCE EQUIPMENT

The Signal Corps used the following radio monitoring sets for radio intelligence:

a. The SCR-243 and 244 were low, middle, and high _requency intercept receivers. Frequency ranges were 100 kilocycles (kc) to 20 megacycles (mc).

b. The SCR-607, 612, 613, 614, and 616 were receivers for frequencies ranging from 15kc to 600mc. They were used to collect continuous wave (CW), AM and FM types of signals.

c. The SCR-558 was a combined intercept and DF assembly. It consisted of an SCR-206 and SCR-504, intercept receiver SCR-612, and communication radio SCR-284. The whole assembly fit within one vehicle.

d. The AN/VRD-1 was a larger assembly, embracing the direction finding SCR-503, intercept receivers SCR-612 and 613, and radio beacon RC-163. The whole assembly took two vehicles, each carrying an SCR-510 to communicate with the other.

GLOSSARY

COMSEC - Communications Security

COMMZ - Communication Zone

DF- Direction Finding

ETO - European Theater of Operations

ETOUSA - European Theater of Operations, U. S. Army

GHQ - General Headquarters

OCSigO - Office of the Chief Signal Officer.

Generally used at the army group level and above.

Panzer - German armored unit.

Panzer Grenadier - German mechanized or motorized infantry unit

RI - Radio Intelligence. Radio intelligence and signal intelligence are interchangeable terms.

SHAEF - Supreme Headquarters, Allied Expeditionary Force

SIGINT - Signals Intelligence

SIGSEC - Signal Security

SIS - Signal Intelligence Service

SRI - Signal Radio Intelligence

T/O - Table of Organization

TO&E - Table of Organization and Equipment

Trick - Slang term for the intercept section or shift. For example, the first interception section in the intercept platoon would be known as the "First Trick." Schedules would be developed, with each trick conducting intercept operations at a designated period.

Trick Chief - Term representing the Noncommissioned Officer in Charge (NCOIC) of a designated intercept section, or trick.

SELECT BIBLIOGRAPHY

PRIMARY SOURCES

Unpublished Works - Documents

Bethune, P.H. "Report of Observations of Operation Neptune, 8 May-23 July 1944." Memorandum for Assistant Chief of Staff, G-2, Army Ground Forces. (CARL no. 7311)
No mention of Radio Intelligence, its uses, problems with dissemination, etc. LTC Bethune was attached to G-2, V Corps during this period. He observed all phases of intelligence work.
United States Army Service Forces. Memorandum from Signal Corps Ground Signal Agency dated 16 October 1944, Subject: Report on Organization, Operations, and Training of Signal Radio Intelligence Companies in ETOUSA. (CARL no. 4386)

United States Army Service Forces. Memorandum from Signal Corps Ground Signal Agency dated 16 October 1944, Subject: Report on Organization, Operations, and Training of Signal Radio Intelligence Companies in ETOUSA. (Carl no. 4386).

_____. Memorandum from Office of the Chief Signal Officer, Plans and Operations Division. Subject: Report of Trip to Italy - 24 October 1944. (CARL no. 3990)

_____. Signal Corps Engineering Laboratories Memorandum dated 6 August 1945, Subject: Report on Direction Finding Operations in the European Theatre of Operations. (CARL no. 11086)

_____. Memorandum from Office of the Chief Signal Officer dated 24 October 1944, Subject: Employment of Radio Intelligence in Tactical Support of Army and Corps as Observed in Italy 11 May 1944 to 15 August 1944. (CARL no. 5721)

{Those documents found at the Combined Arms Research Library (CARL) are annotated with their file number (e.g., CARL no. 1835). All other material should be at most libraries or available through interlibrary loan programs.}

_____. Memorandum dated 17 May 1944, Subject: AGF Board Report #79, ETO, 118th Sig Radio Intelligence Company. (CARL microfilm)

United States War Department. Memorandum from Office of

the Chief Signal Officer dated 19 April 1945. Subject: PW Intelligence Bulletin No. 2/38 - Signal Intelligence. (CARL no. 8805)

_____. Memorandum from Office of the Chief Signal Officer dated 12 August 1944. Subject: Signal Questionnaire Answered by Signal Radio Intelligence Companies. (CARL no. 7421)

_____. Memorandum from Office of the Chief Signal Officer dated 24 October 1944. Subject: Intercept and its Application. (CARL no. 3569)

_____. Report dated 23 August 1945, Subject: Direction Finder System of the 128th Signal R.I. Co. (CARL no. 12615)

_____. Memorandum from Office of the Chief Signal Officer dated June 2, 1943. Subject: Observers' Reports, 1943 maneuvers. (CARL no. 1835).

_____. Memorandum from Office of the Chief Signal Officer dated 22 June 1943. Subject: Observers' Reports, 1943 maneuvers. (CARL no. 1835).

12th Army Group. Report of Operations (Final After Action Report) (12 vols), vol III - G-2 Section; vol IX -Headquarters Commandant Section and Special Troops; vol XI Antiaircraft Artillery, Armored, Artillery, Signal and Chemical Warfare Sections. 1945?

_____. "History, Signal Section, 12th Army Group (FUSAG)," Historical Documents World War II. AGO Microfilm; Job No. 500, reel No. 115, item 1339.

Third United States Army. After Action Report Third US Army 1 August 1944 - 9 May 1945: vol II Staff Section Reports. 1945?

V Corps Historical Section. V Corps in the ETO, 6 January 1942 - 9 May 1945.

116th Signal Radio Intelligence Company. History of the 116th Signal Radio Intelligence Company from Date of Activation, 18 May, 1942 until V-J Day, 2 September, 1945. Munich: R. Oldenbourg, 1945.

Excellent history of the unit from the soldier's viewpoint. Does not contain any technical data, nor a review of their intelligence successes or failures. Instead, it provides a human dimension to the training, hopes and fears of intelligence personnel during World War II.

American Expeditionary Forces, General Staff, Second Section. "Final Report of the Radio Intelligence Section, General Staff, General Headquarters, American Expeditionary Forces, 1918-1919." File SRH-014, Records of the National Security Agency, National Archives Record Group #457.

Army Security Agency. "Examples of Intelligence Obtained from Cryptanalsis, 1 August 1946." File SRH-066, Records of the National Security Agency, National Archives Control Number NN3-457-81-3. Reprinted in US Army Command and General Staff College, A627 Book of Readings, 125-137. Ft Leavenworth, KS: US Army Command and General Staff College, 1982.

_____. "Historical Background of the Signal Security Agency (3 vols); Volume II: World War I; Volume III: The Peace (1919-1939)." File SRH-001, Records of the National Security Agency, National Archives Record Group #457.

_____. "Histories of Radio Intelligence Units, European Theater, September 1944 to March 1945." File SRH-228, Records of the National Security Agency, National Archives Control Number NN3-457-83-34.

Friedman, William F. "A Brief History of the Signal Intelligence Service." dated June 29, 1942. File SRH-029, Records of the National Security Agency, National Archives Record Group #457.

Good account of beginning of the Signal Intelligence Service. Follows mostly the cryptanalysis and breaking of the Japanese codes in late 1930s. No mention of operational or tactical radio intercept; stays mainly with strategic/national level.

Third United States Army Signal Intelligence Service. "Third Army Radio Intelligence History in Campaign of Western Europe." SRH-042, Records of the National Security Agency, National Archives Record Group #457. This document is also included in SRH-228.

Traite De Paix Entre Les Puissances Allides Et Associees Et L'Allemagne Et Protocole Signes A Versailles, Le 28 Juin 1919. From the collection of Dr S.J. Lewis, US Army Command and General Staff College, Fort Leavenworth, KS.

United States War Department. Table of Organization no. 11-77 Signal Radio Intelligence Company. Washington, DC: US Government Printing Office, 1942.

_____. Table of Organization no. 11-500 Signal Service Organization. Washington, DC: US Government Printing Office, 1943.

Yardley, Herbert 0. "A History of the Code and Cipher Section During the First World War (prepared in 1919)." File SRH-030, Records of the National Security Agency, National Archives Record Group #457. Yardley's account of the history of MI-8 during World War I, as edited by William F. Friedman. While the disclaimer is that the text is reproduced as originally written, Friedman, as the editor, does not have any problems skewering Yardley. Friedman's footnotes to Yardley's accounts show his dislike of Yardley and the early history of MI-8 prior to the organization of the Signal Security Agency. Interesting from a personal standpoint to'\see the friction between two of the more important persons in the history of signals intelligence.

Books

Behrendt, Hans-Otto. Rommel's Intelligence in the Desert Campaign. London: William Kimber, 1985.
Excellent overview of intelligence during the North African campaign. Behrendt is able to provide first person experience of Rommel's success. Good overview of the importance of Signal Intelligence, as well as the other "ints" to Rommel.

Clayton, Aileen. The Enemy is Listening. New York: Ballantine Books, 1982.

Flicke, Wilhelm F. War Secrets in the Ether (2 vols). Laguna Hills, CA: Aegean Park Press, 1977.

Koch, Oscar W. G-2: Intelligence for Patton. Philadelphia: Whitmore Publishing Co., 1971.

Military Intelligence Division, U.S. War Department. German Military Intelligence 1939-1945. Frederick, MD: University Publications of America, 1984.

Praun, Albert. "German Radio Intelligence (Foreign Military Studies Manuscript P-038)." In German Radio Intelligenge and the Soldatensender (Covert Warfare, No. 6),, ed. John M. Mendelsohn. New York: Garland Publishing, Inc., 1989.

United States War Department. Handbook on German Military Forces. Baton Rouge, LA: Louisiana State University Press, 1990.

Yardley, Herbert 0. The American Black Chamber. New York: Ballantine Books, 1981.

Articles

Black, Garland C., Captain, "The G-2 Signals Team." The Signal Corps Bulletin 90 (May-June 1936): 24-42.

Hamlin, W.D., Captain, "Organization and Training of the Third Radio Intelligence Company." The Signal Corps Bulletin 108 (April-June 1940): 127-29.

Rosengarten, Aldolph G., Jr. "With Ultra from Omaha Beach to Weimar,Germany - A Personal View." Military Affairs XLII (October 1978): 127-133.

United States Army, Office of the Chief Signal Officer. "New TO and E Includes Functional Teams and Team Equipment." Signal Corps Technical Information Letter 23 (October 1943): 75-76.

_____. "Radio Direction Finding Central TC-8 and Radio Intercept Central TC-9." 5ignal Corps Technical Information Letter 27 (February 1944): 49-55.

_____. "Frequency Coverage, Tactical Radio Sets." Signal Corps Technical Information Letter 32 (July 1944): 32-33.

_____."Signal Corps Board; Cases Approved by the Chief Signal Officer; Case No. 523, Supplement 1 - Service Test of Improved Loop Assembly AS-4/GR." Signal Corps Technical Information Letter 33 (August 1944): 37.

_____. "Radio Intelligence Operations." Signal Corps Technical Information Letter 34 September 1944): 9-10,23.

_____. "Radio Control Center." Signal Corps Technical Information Letter 36 (November 1944): 13-14.

_____. "Direction Finders." Signal Corps Technical Information Letter 37 (December 1944): 7-10.

Field Manuals

United States Department of the Army. FM 100-5: Operations. Washington, DC: US Government Printing Office, 1986.

_____. FM 11-65: High Frequency Communications. Washington, DC; October 1978.

_____. FM, 30-476: Radio Direction Finding Operations. Washington, DC; April 1977.

_____. Historical Division. United States Army in the World War 1917-1919: Organization of the American Expeditionary Forces. Washington, DC: US Government Printing Office, 1948.

_____. Historical Division. United States Army in the World War 1917-1919: Reports of Commander-in-Chief. A.E.F., Staff Sections and Services. Washington, DC: US Government Printing Office, 1948.

_____. DA Pamphlet 672-1. Unit Citation and Campaign Participation Register. Washington, DC; July 1961.

United States Signal Corps. Signal Corps Field Manual, Volume I - Signal Corps Troops. Washington, DC US Government Printing Office, 1931.

_____. Signal Corps Field Manual. Volume II - Signal Corps

<u>Operations.</u> Washington, DC: US Government Printing Office, 1931.

United States School of the Line. <u>Signal Communication for all Arms.</u> Fort Leavenworth, KS, The General Service Schools Press, 1922.

United States War Department. <u>FM 100-5, Field Service Regulations-Operations.</u> Washington, DC: War Department, 1941; reprint, Ft. Leavenworth: USACGSC Press, 1992.

_____. <u>FM 11-20: Signal Corps Field Manual Organization and Operations in the Corps. Army, Theater of Operations, and GHO.</u> Washington, DC: War Department, 1940.

_____. <u>FM 11-22; Signal Operations to the Corps and Army.</u> Washington, DC: War Department, 1945.

SECONDARY SOURCES

Unpublished Material - Manuscripts

Burgess, Ronald L. <u>Equipment. Organization and Command and Control Relationships of Intelligence and Electronic Warfare Support to the Heavy Division.</u> Ft Leavenworth, KS: School of Advanced Military Studies, US Army Command and General Staff College, 1986.

Gribble, Jr., G. Dickson. <u>ULTRA: Its Operational Use in the</u>

European Theater of Operations. 1943-1945. Carlisle Barracks, PA: US Army War College, 1991.

Excellent overview of ULTRA at the army group and army level. Identifies the roles the Special Liaison Units (SLUs) in providing intelligence to the operational commander. Does not discuss radio intelligence units at army group, army, or corps level.

Horgan, Penelope S. Signals Intelligence Support to U.S. Military Commanders: Past and Present. Carlisle Barracks, PA: U.S. Army War College, 1991.

Millet, John D. The ASF (Army Service Forces] in World War II, December 1941 - 1945. Unpublished manuscript on Center Of Military History Microfilm reels 34 and 35, document number 3-1.1A AA. Washington DC: Center of Military History unpublished manuscript,. 1945.

Reame, A.G. Electronic Warfare in the Field Army: A Historical Analysis. Ft Leavenworth, KS: US Army Command and General Staff College, 1964. (MMAS Thesis - CARL no. 13423.344-A-2)

Published Material

Books

Army Security Agency. The Origin and Development of the Army Security Agency 1917-1947 [Washington. DC: march 1948). Laguna Hills, CA: Aegean Park Press, 1978.

Beringer, Richard E., Herman Hattaway, Archer Jones, and William N. Still, Jr. Why the South Lost the Civil War. Athens, GA, University of Georgia Press, 1986.

Bidwell, Bruce W. History of the Military Intelligence Division. Department of the Army General Staff: 1775-1941. Frederick, MD: University Publications of America, Inc., 1986. An excellent study of the development of military intelligence from 1775-1941; however, there is little mention of radio or signals intelligence.

Blumenson, Martin. The Patton Papers; 1940-1945. Boston, Houghton Mifflin Company, 1974.

Calvocoressi, Peter. Top Secret ULTRA. New York: Ballantine Books, 1981.

Finnegan, John Patrick. Military Intelligence: A Picture History. Arlington, VA, History Office, US Army Intelligence and Security Command, 1984. Pictorial history of intelligence from the late 1880s to present day. Very interesting, especially in the early time.

Gabel, Christopher R. The Lorraine Campaign: An Overview, September-December 1944. Ft Leavenworth, KS: U.S. Army Command and General Staff College, 1985.

Griffin, Gary B. The Directed Telescope: A Traditional Element of Effective Command. 1985. Reprint. Ft Leavenworth, KS: U.S. Army Command and General Staff College, 1991.

Griffith, Samuel B., trans. Sun Tzu: The Art of War. London: Oxford University Press, 1963.

Hinsley, F. H. British Intelligence in the Second World War: Its Influence on Strategy and Operations (Volume Two). New York: Cambridge University Press, 1981.

_____. British Intelligence in the Second World War: Its Influence on Strategy and Operations (Volume Three, Part II). New York: Cambridge University Press, 1988.

House, Johathan M. Toward Combined Arms Warfare: A Survey of 20th-Century Tactics, Doctrine. And Organization. Ft Leavenworth, KS: U.S. Army Command and General Staff College, 1984.

Kahn, David. Hitler's Spies: German Military Intelligence, in World War II. New York: MacMillan publishing Co., 1978.

Keegan, John. The Second World War. New York: Penguin

Books, USA Inc., 1990.

Munro, Neil. The Quick and the Dead: Electronic Combat and Modern Warfare. New York: St. Martin's Press, 1991.

Norman, Bruce. Secret Warfare: The Battle of Codes and Ciphers. Davis & Charles (Publishers) Ltd., 1973; New York: Dorset Press, 1987.

Paine, Lauran. German Military Intelligence in World War II. The Abwehr. Stein & Day, 1984; New York: Military Heritage Press, 1988.

Pratt, Fletcher. Secret and Urgent - The Story of Codes and Ciphers. New York: The Bobbs -Merrill Company, 1939.

Spector, Ronald H. Listening to the Enemy. Wilmington, DE: Scholary Resources, Inc., 1988. Collection of documents pertaining to MAGIC. Nothing relating to radio intelligence units.

Terrett, Dulany. The Signal Corps: The Emergency (To December 1941). Washington, DC: Center of Military History, 1986.

Thompson, George R., Dixie R. Harris, Pauline M. Oakes, and Dulany Terrett. The Signals Corps: The Test (December 1941 To July 19431. Washington, DC: Office of the Chief of Military History, 1957.

Thompson, George R. and Dixie R. Harris. The Signal

Corps: The Outcome (Mid 1943 Through 1945). Washington, DC: Office of the Chief of Military History, 1966.

Toppe, Alfred. Desert Warfare: German Experiences in World War II. Ft Leavenworth, KS: U.S. Army Command and General Staff College, 1991.

Tuchman, Barbara W. The Guns of August. New York: MacMillan Publishing Co., Inc., 1962; Bantam Books, 1980.

West, Nigel. The SIGINT Secrets: The Signals Intelligence War. 1900 to Today. New York: William Morrow and Company, Inc., 1988.

Whiting, Charles. Ardennes: The Secret War. Stein & Day, 1984; New York: Dorset Press, 1987.

Articles

Angevine, Robert G. "Gentlemen Do Read Each Other's Mail: American Intelligence in the Interwar Era." Intelligence and National Security 7, no 2 (1992): 1-29.

Bigelow, Michael E., Captain. "Big Business: Intelligence in Patton's Third Army." Military Intelligence. 18, no. 2 (April-June 1992): 31-36.

Hooker, C.E., Major, "Signals Intelligence." Canadian Defence Quarterly 19, no. 2 (October 1989): 50-59.

Kahn, David. "German Military Eavesdroppers." <u>Cryptologia</u> (October 1977): 378-380.

Riccardelli, Richard, Major, "Electronic Warfare in WWII." <u>Army Communicator</u> 10, no. 1 (Winter 1985): 40-49.

Stewart, Richard A., Major, "Rommel's Secret Weapon: Signals Intelligence." <u>Marine Corps Gazette</u> 74, no. 3 (March 1990): 51-55.

www.ingramcontent.com/pod-product-compliance
Lightning Source LLC
Chambersburg PA
CBHW070903290526
45795CB00001B/220